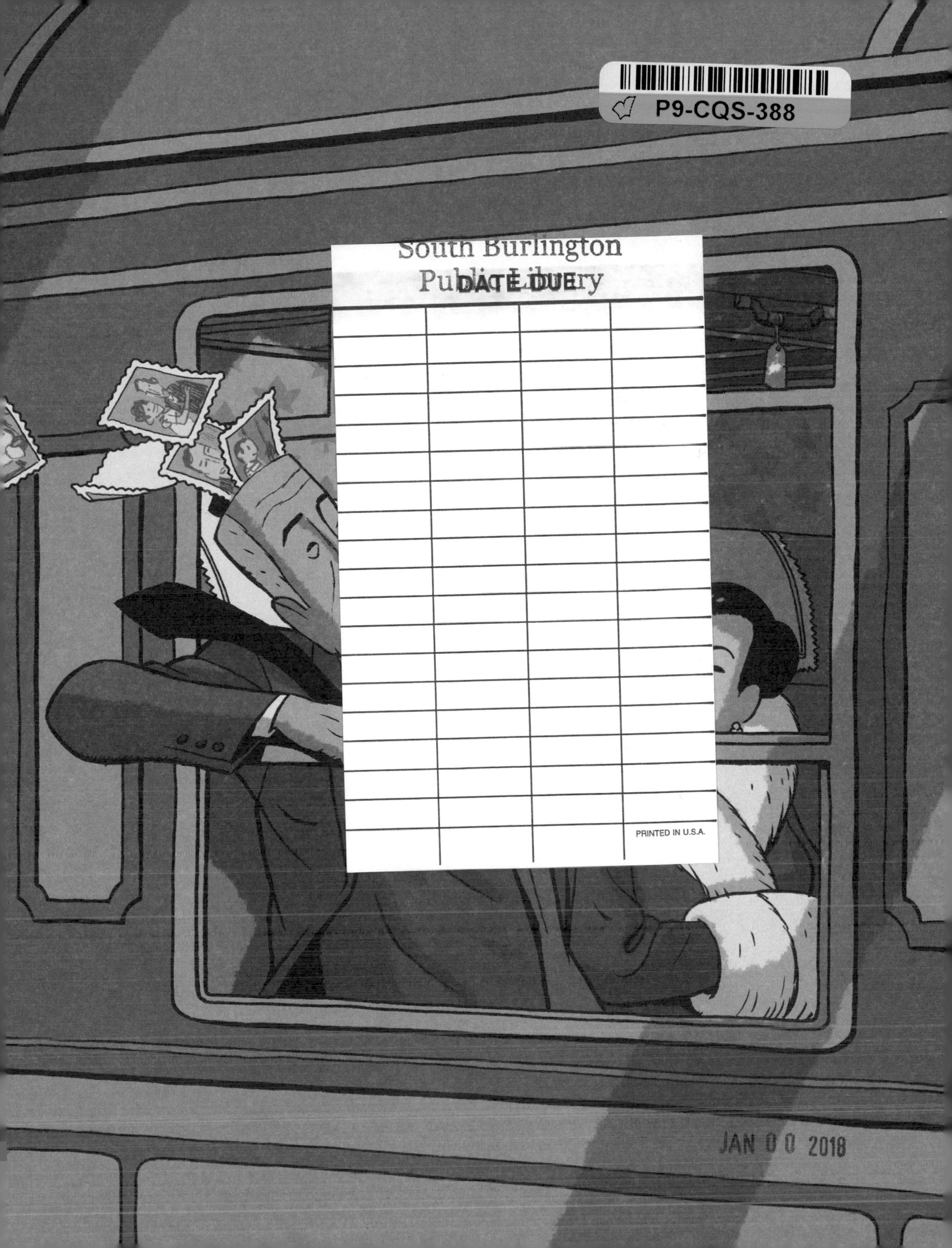

Wrinkles

Publisher: GARY GROTH
Fantagraphics Editor: J. MICHAEL CATRON
Fantagraphics Designer: MICHAEL HECK
Translator: ERICA MENA
Associate Publisher: ERIC REYNOLDS

Fantagraphics Books, Inc.
7563 Lake City Way NE
Seattle, WA 98115
(800) 657-1100

Fantagraphics.com. • Twitter: @fantagraphics • facebook.com/fantagraphics

First Fantagraphics Books edition: August 2016

ISBN 978-1-60699-932-5
Library of Congress Control Number: 2016930071
Printed in China

PACO ROCA

Wrinkles

Fantagraphics Books
Seattle

For my parents

"The clouds do not disappear, they turn into rain."

— Buddha

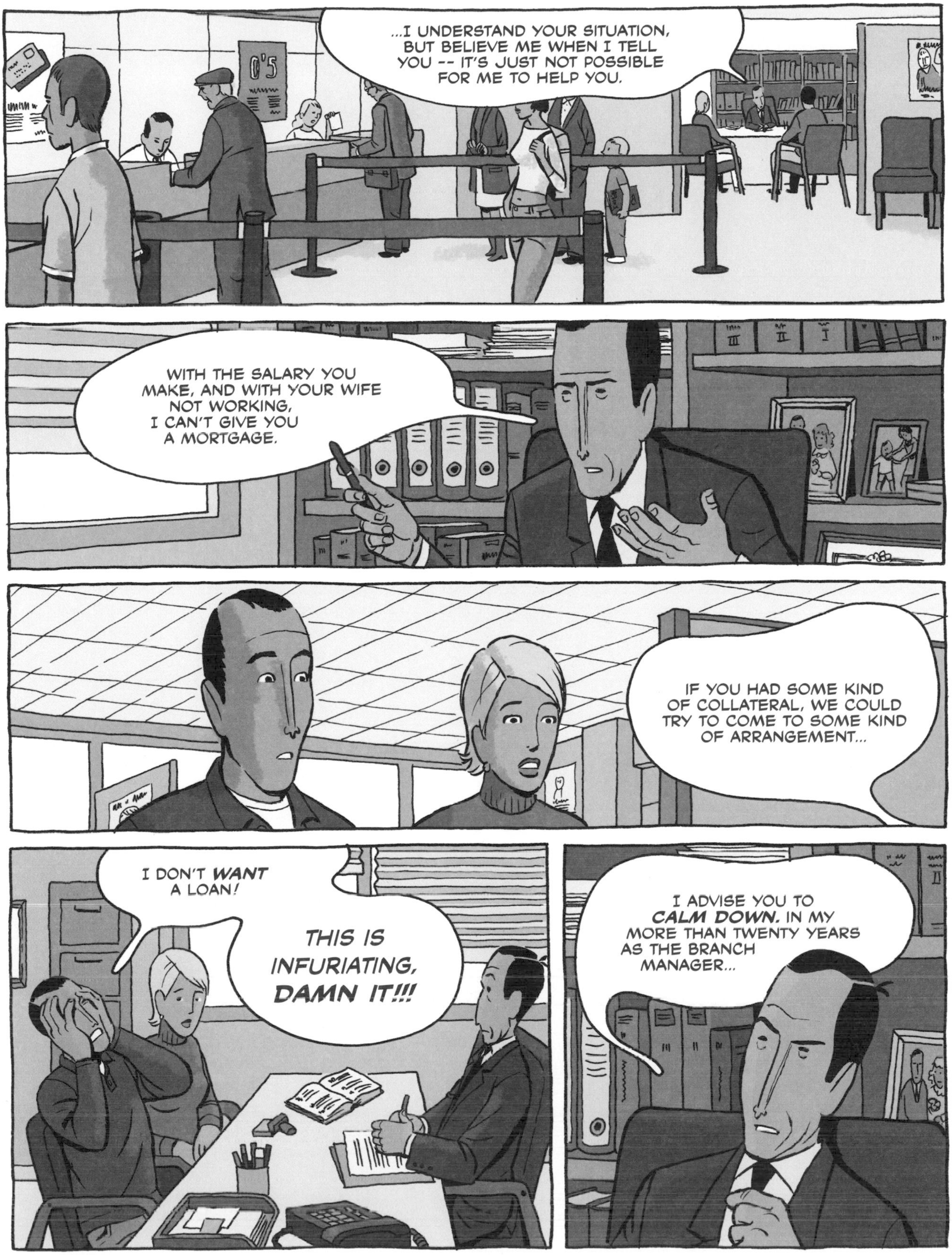
...I UNDERSTAND YOUR SITUATION, BUT BELIEVE ME WHEN I TELL YOU -- IT'S JUST NOT POSSIBLE FOR ME TO HELP YOU.
WITH THE SALARY YOU MAKE, AND WITH YOUR WIFE NOT WORKING, I CAN'T GIVE YOU A MORTGAGE.
IF YOU HAD SOME KIND OF COLLATERAL, WE COULD TRY TO COME TO SOME KIND OF ARRANGEMENT...
I DON'T *WANT* A LOAN!
THIS IS INFURIATING, ***DAMN IT!!!***
I ADVISE YOU TO ***CALM DOWN.*** IN MY MORE THAN TWENTY YEARS AS THE BRANCH MANAGER...

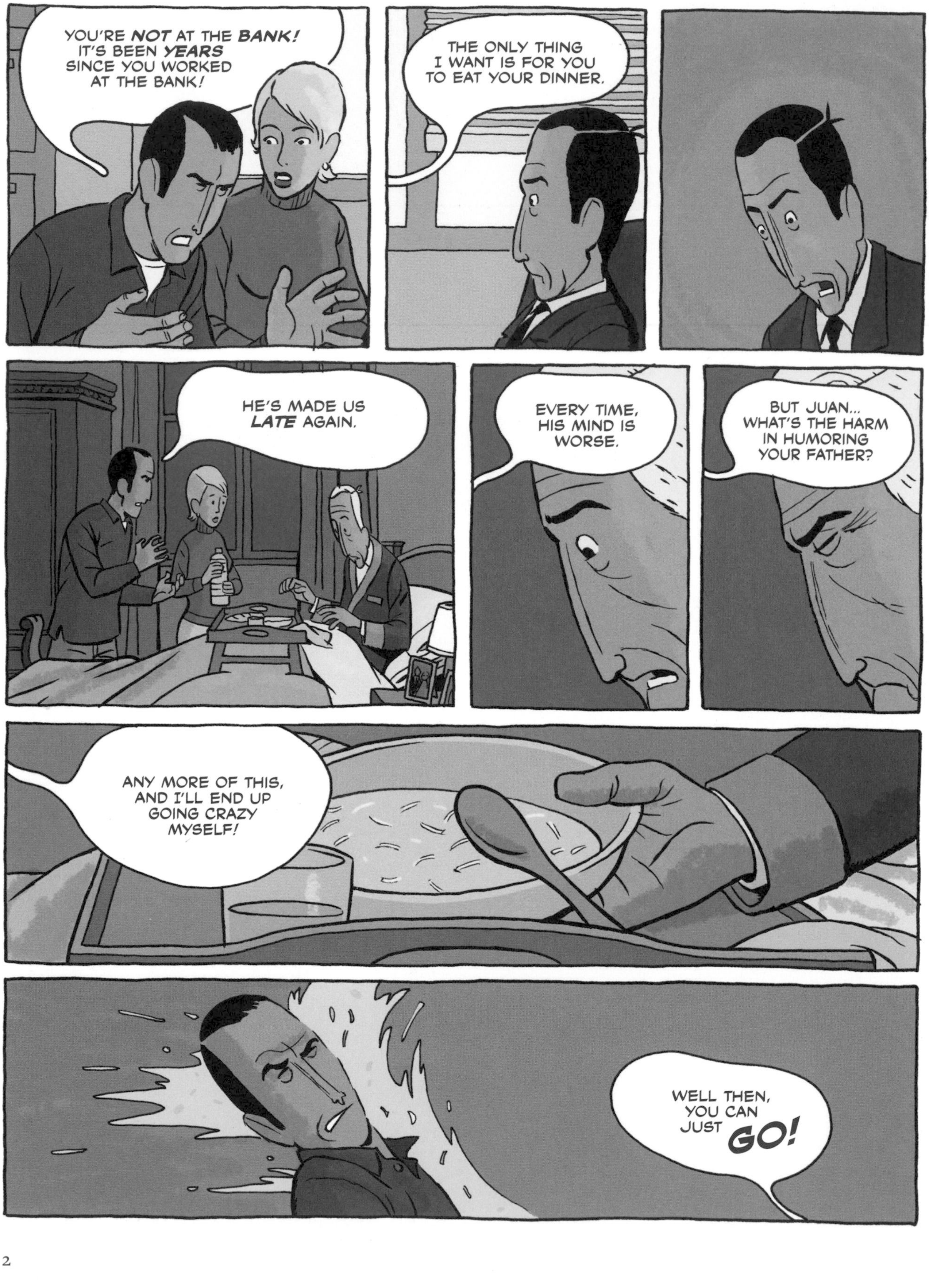
YOU'RE NOT AT THE BANK! IT'S BEEN YEARS SINCE YOU WORKED AT THE BANK!
THE ONLY THING I WANT IS FOR YOU TO EAT YOUR DINNER.
HE'S MADE US LATE AGAIN.
EVERY TIME, HIS MIND IS WORSE.
BUT JUAN... WHAT'S THE HARM IN HUMORING YOUR FATHER?
ANY MORE OF THIS, AND I'LL END UP GOING CRAZY MYSELF!
WELL THEN, YOU CAN JUST GO!

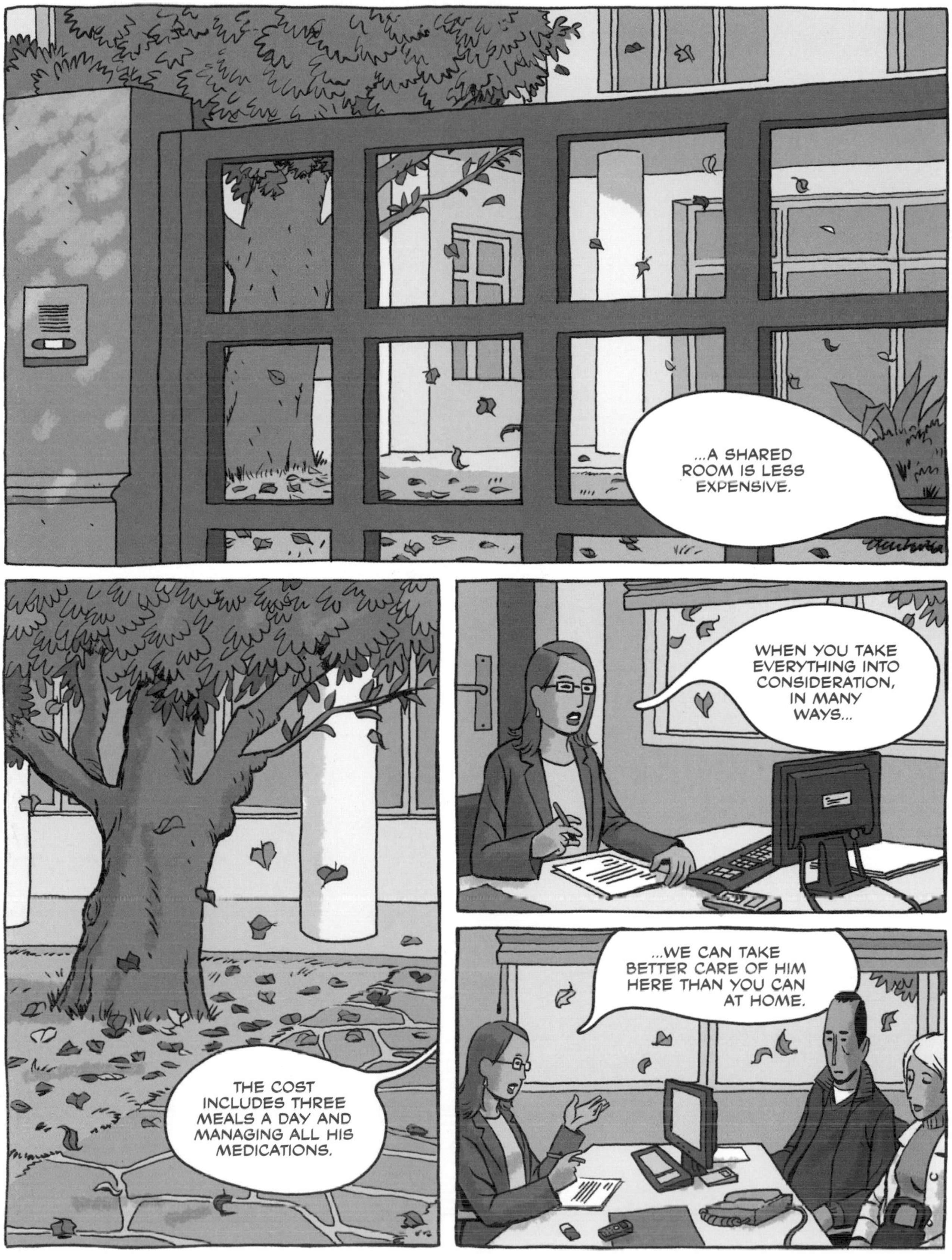
...A SHARED ROOM IS LESS EXPENSIVE.
THE COST INCLUDES THREE MEALS A DAY AND MANAGING ALL HIS MEDICATIONS.
WHEN YOU TAKE EVERYTHING INTO CONSIDERATION, IN MANY WAYS...
...WE CAN TAKE BETTER CARE OF HIM HERE THAN YOU CAN AT HOME.

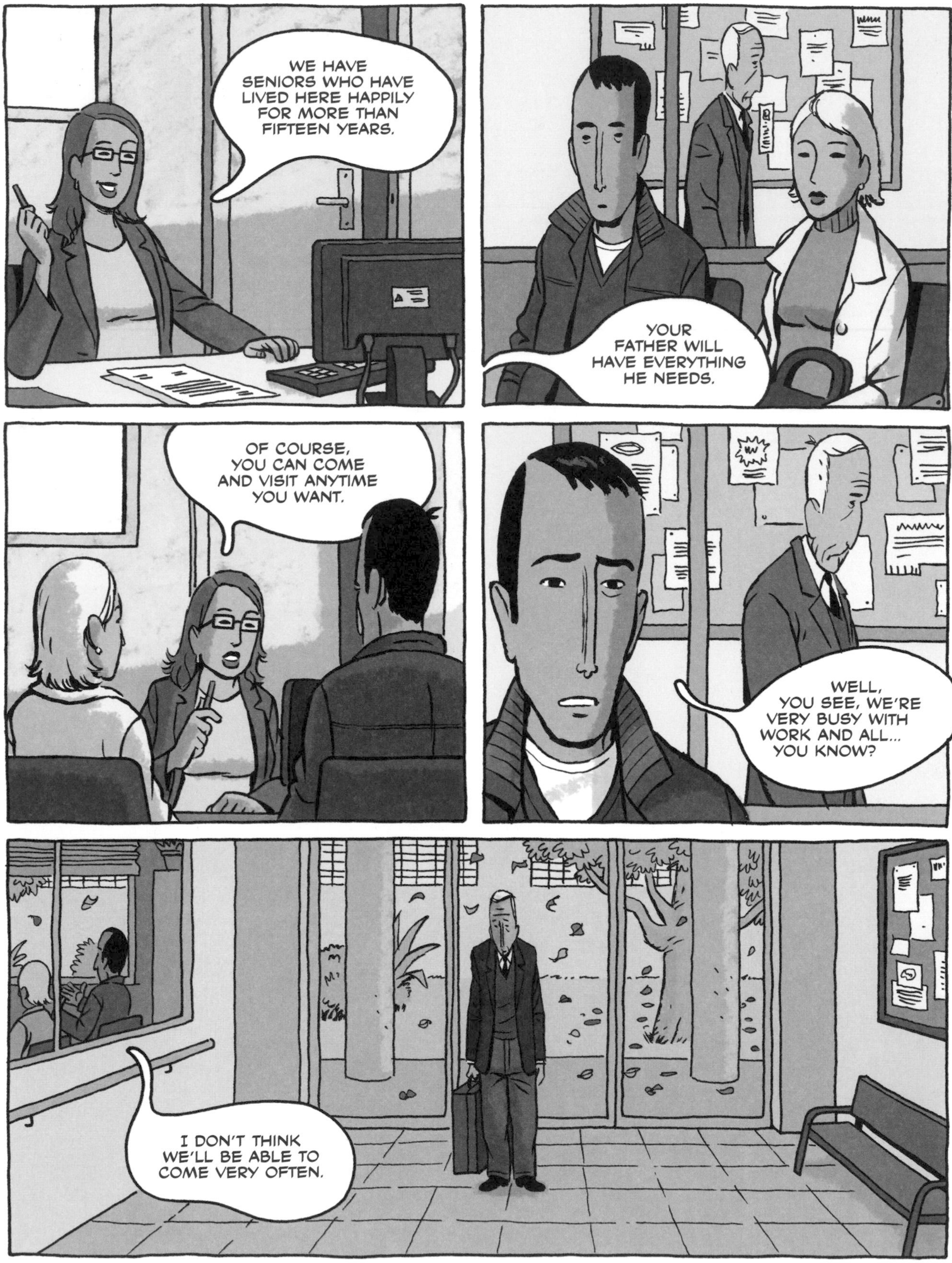
WE HAVE SENIORS WHO HAVE LIVED HERE HAPPILY FOR MORE THAN FIFTEEN YEARS.
YOUR FATHER WILL HAVE EVERYTHING HE NEEDS.
OF COURSE, YOU CAN COME AND VISIT ANYTIME YOU WANT.
WELL, YOU SEE, WE'RE VERY BUSY WITH WORK AND ALL... YOU KNOW?
I DON'T THINK WE'LL BE ABLE TO COME VERY OFTEN.

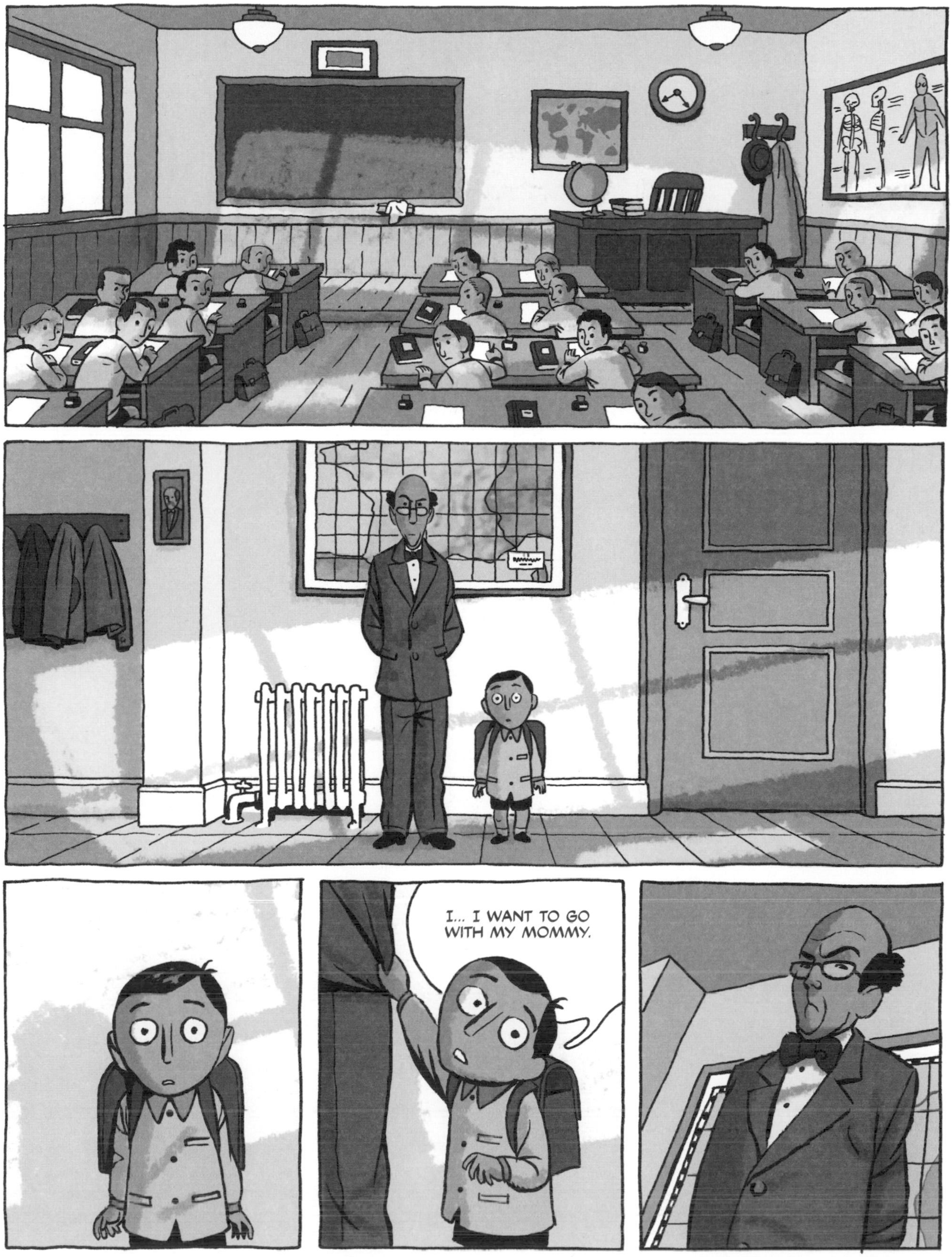
I... I WANT TO GO WITH MY MOMMY.

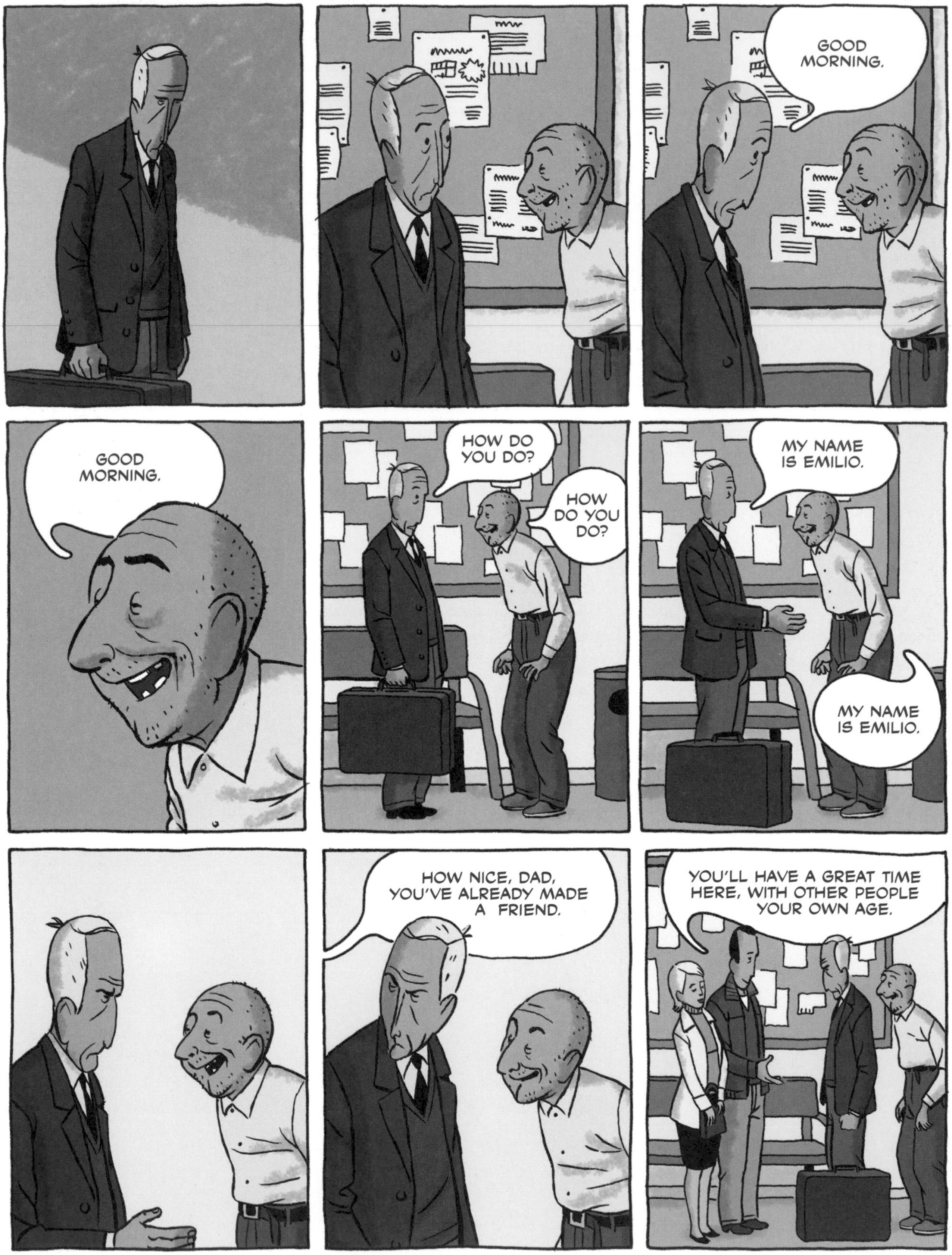
GOOD MORNING.
GOOD MORNING.
HOW DO YOU DO?
HOW DO YOU DO?
MY NAME IS EMILIO.
MY NAME IS EMILIO.
HOW NICE, DAD, YOU'VE ALREADY MADE A FRIEND.
YOU'LL HAVE A GREAT TIME HERE, WITH OTHER PEOPLE YOUR OWN AGE.

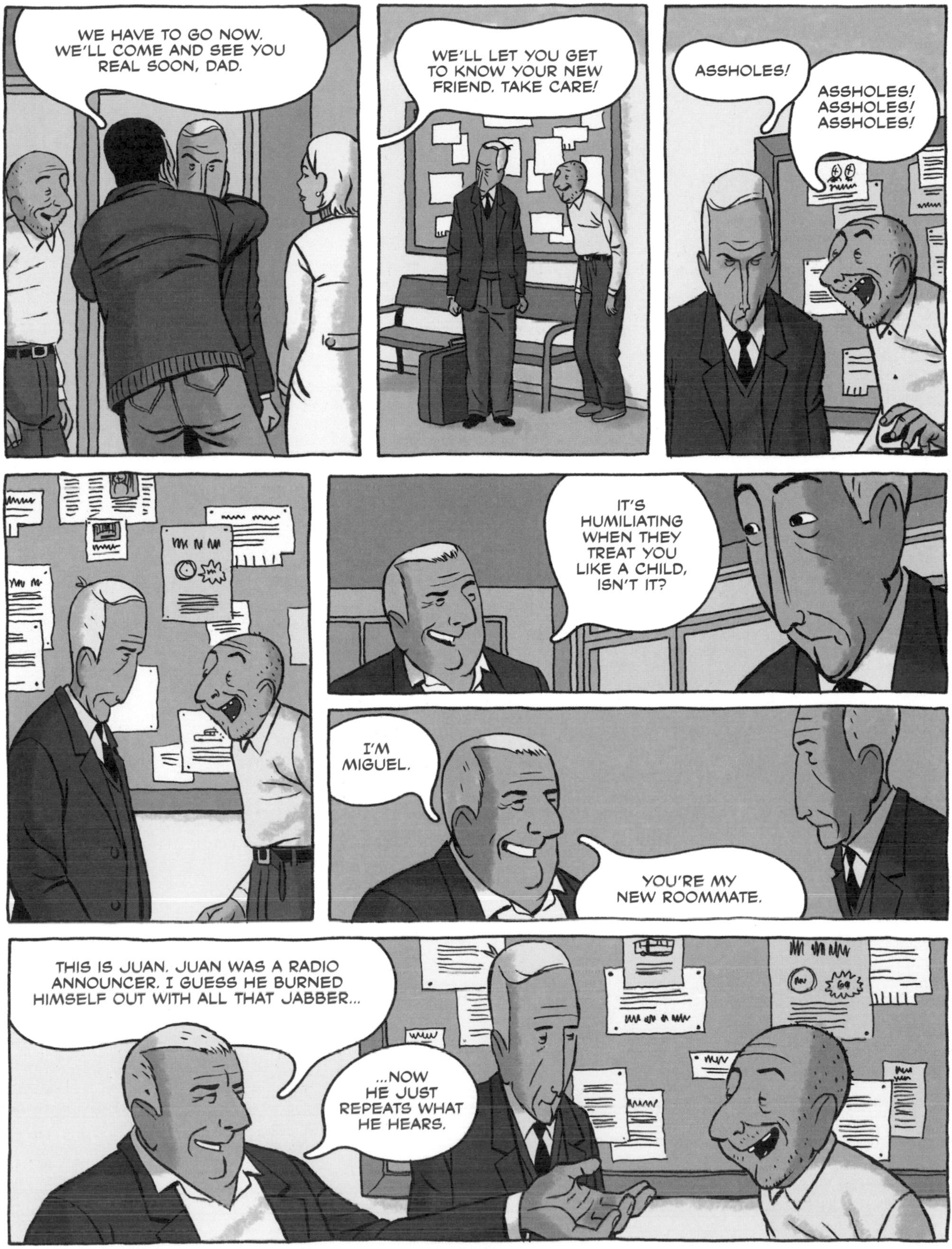
WE HAVE TO GO NOW. WE'LL COME AND SEE YOU REAL SOON, DAD.
WE'LL LET YOU GET TO KNOW YOUR NEW FRIEND. TAKE CARE!
ASSHOLES!
ASSHOLES! ASSHOLES! ASSHOLES!
IT'S HUMILIATING WHEN THEY TREAT YOU LIKE A CHILD, ISN'T IT?
I'M MIGUEL.
YOU'RE MY NEW ROOMMATE.
THIS IS JUAN. JUAN WAS A RADIO ANNOUNCER. I GUESS HE BURNED HIMSELF OUT WITH ALL THAT JABBER...
...NOW HE JUST REPEATS WHAT HE HEARS.

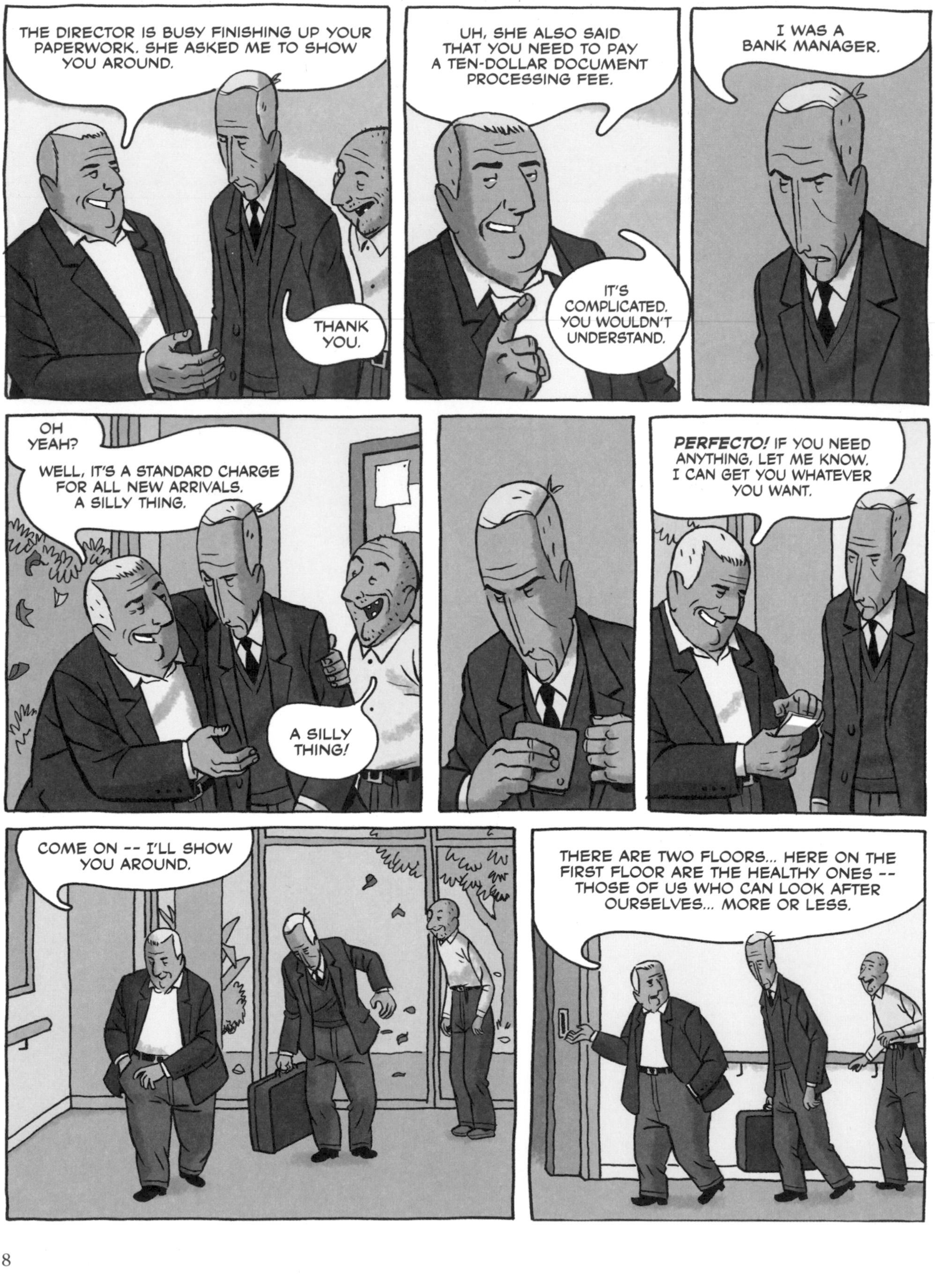
THE DIRECTOR IS BUSY FINISHING UP YOUR PAPERWORK. SHE ASKED ME TO SHOW YOU AROUND.
THANK YOU.
UH, SHE ALSO SAID THAT YOU NEED TO PAY A TEN-DOLLAR DOCUMENT PROCESSING FEE.
IT'S COMPLICATED. YOU WOULDN'T UNDERSTAND.
I WAS A BANK MANAGER.
OH YEAH?
WELL, IT'S A STANDARD CHARGE FOR ALL NEW ARRIVALS. A SILLY THING.
A SILLY THING!
PERFECTO! IF YOU NEED ANYTHING, LET ME KNOW. I CAN GET YOU WHATEVER YOU WANT.
COME ON -- I'LL SHOW YOU AROUND.
THERE ARE TWO FLOORS... HERE ON THE FIRST FLOOR ARE THE HEALTHY ONES -- THOSE OF US WHO CAN LOOK AFTER OURSELVES... MORE OR LESS.

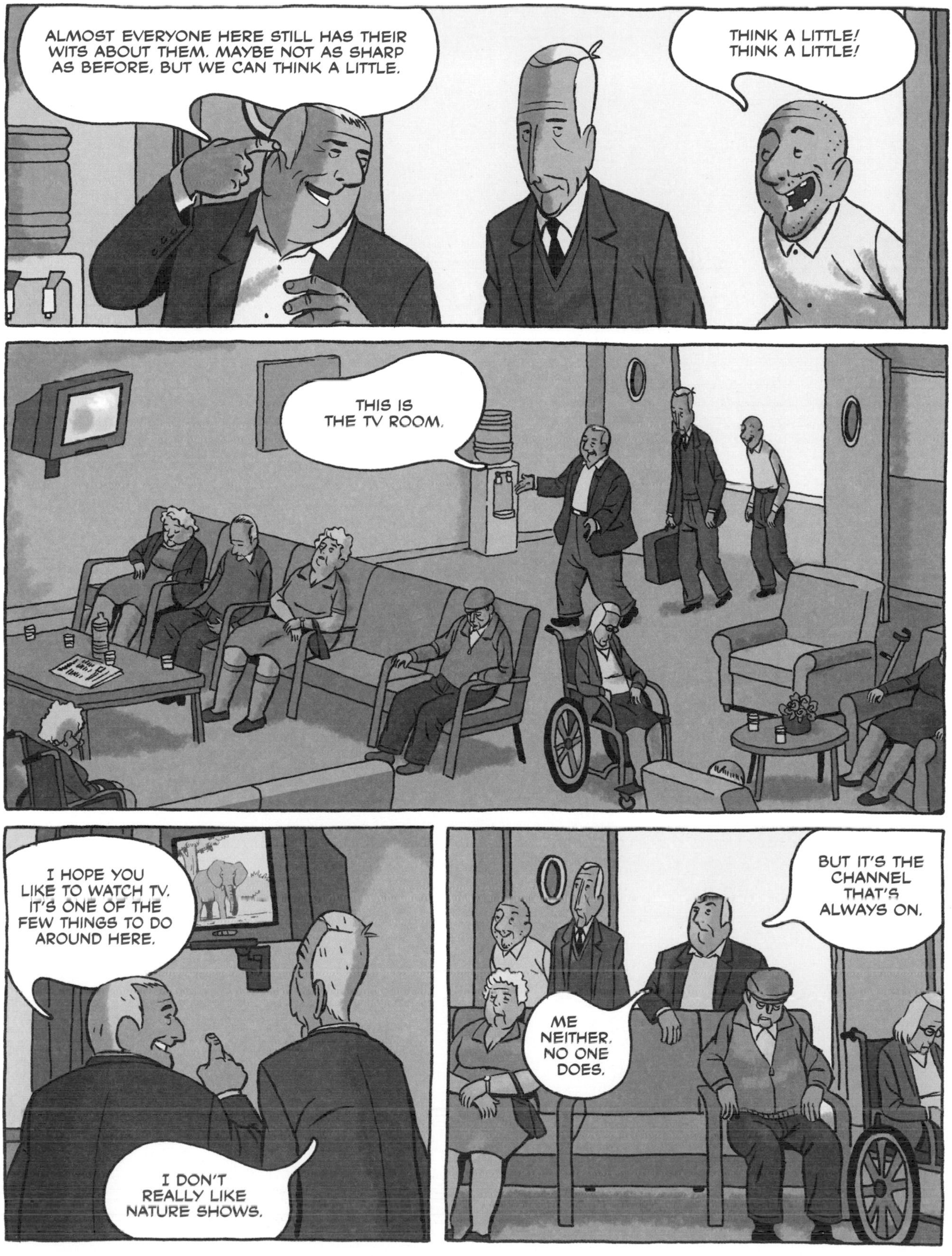
ALMOST EVERYONE HERE STILL HAS THEIR WITS ABOUT THEM. MAYBE NOT AS SHARP AS BEFORE, BUT WE CAN THINK A LITTLE.
THINK A LITTLE! THINK A LITTLE!
THIS IS THE TV ROOM.
I HOPE YOU LIKE TO WATCH TV. IT'S ONE OF THE FEW THINGS TO DO AROUND HERE.
I DON'T REALLY LIKE NATURE SHOWS.
BUT IT'S THE CHANNEL THAT'S ALWAYS ON.
ME NEITHER. NO ONE DOES.

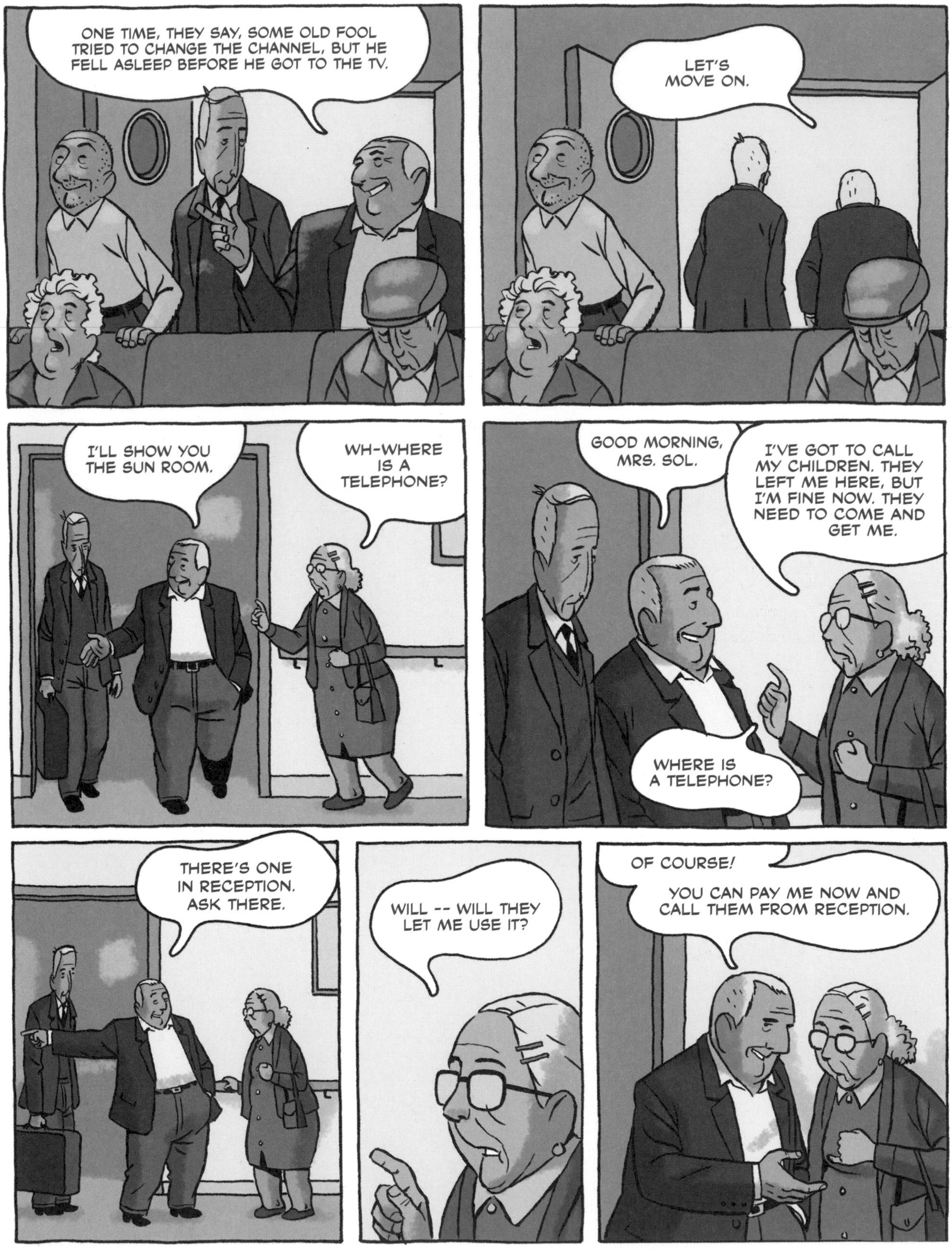
ONE TIME, THEY SAY, SOME OLD FOOL TRIED TO CHANGE THE CHANNEL, BUT HE FELL ASLEEP BEFORE HE GOT TO THE TV.
LET'S MOVE ON.
I'LL SHOW YOU THE SUN ROOM.
WH-WHERE IS A TELEPHONE?
GOOD MORNING, MRS. SOL.
I'VE GOT TO CALL MY CHILDREN. THEY LEFT ME HERE, BUT I'M FINE NOW. THEY NEED TO COME AND GET ME.
WHERE IS A TELEPHONE?
THERE'S ONE IN RECEPTION. ASK THERE.
WILL -- WILL THEY LET ME USE IT?
OF COURSE!
YOU CAN PAY ME NOW AND CALL THEM FROM RECEPTION.

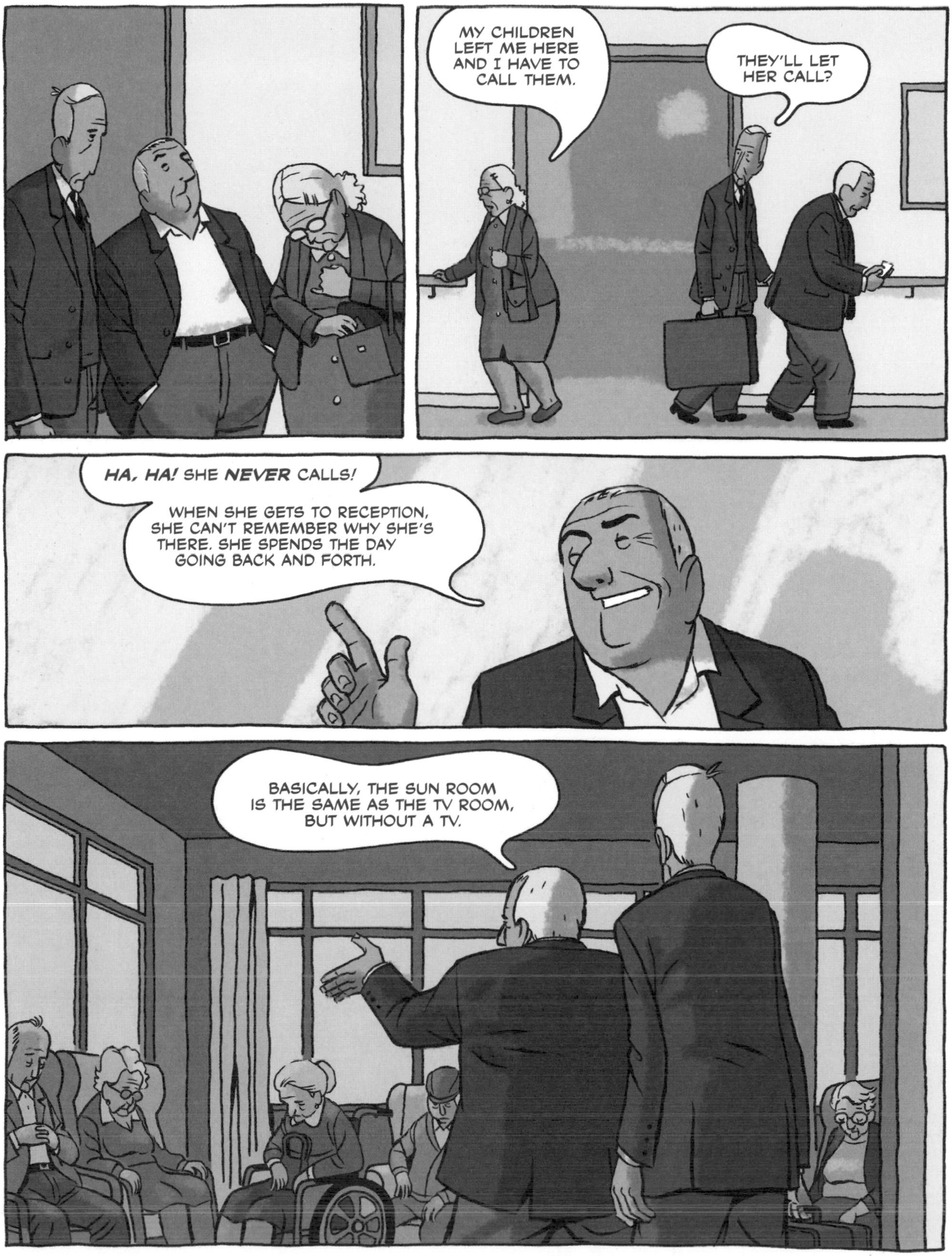
MY CHILDREN LEFT ME HERE AND I HAVE TO CALL THEM.
THEY'LL LET HER CALL?
HA, HA! SHE **NEVER** CALLS!
WHEN SHE GETS TO RECEPTION, SHE CAN'T REMEMBER WHY SHE'S THERE. SHE SPENDS THE DAY GOING BACK AND FORTH.
BASICALLY, THE SUN ROOM IS THE SAME AS THE TV ROOM, BUT WITHOUT A TV.

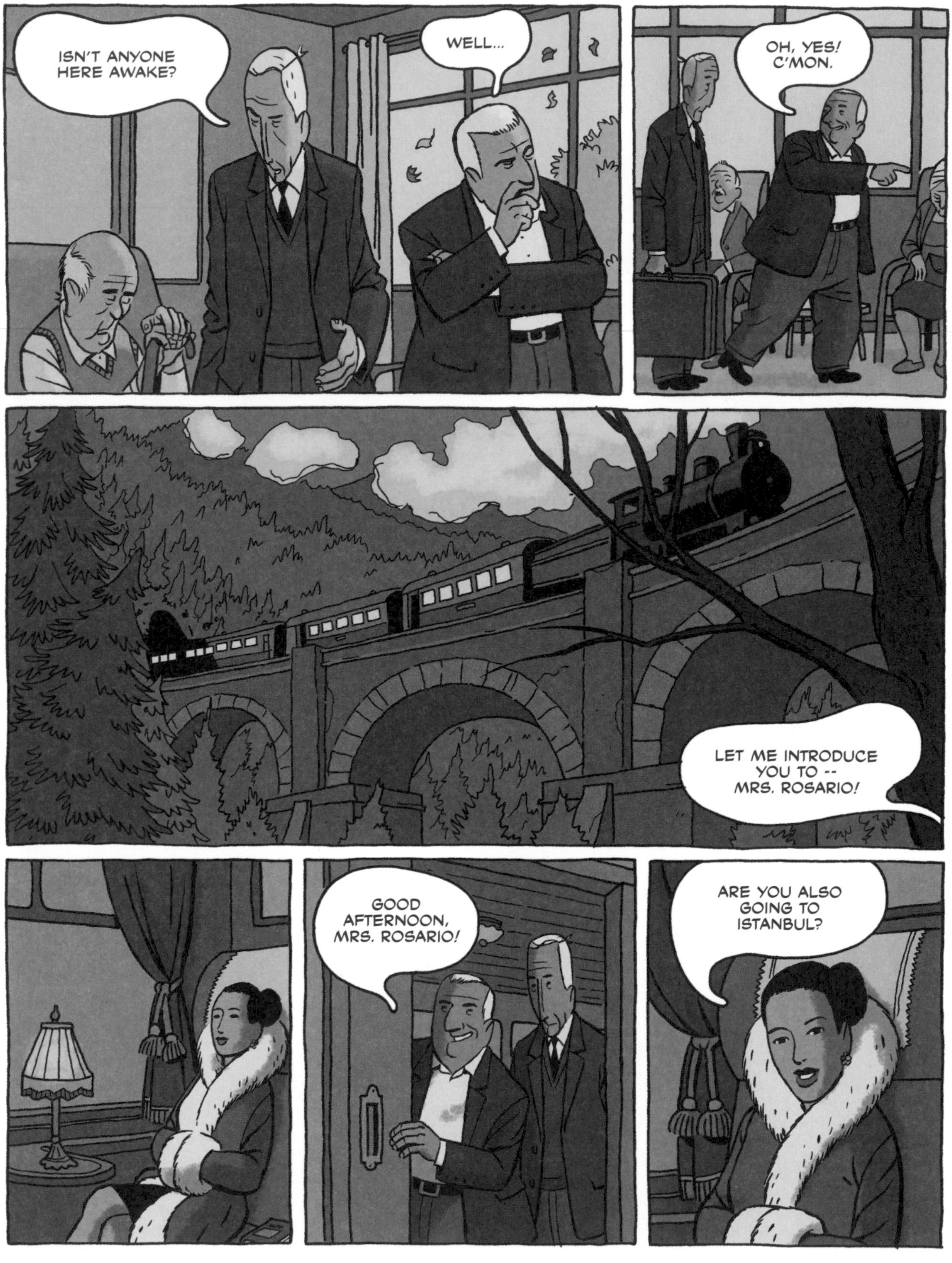
ISN'T ANYONE HERE AWAKE?
WELL...
OH, YES! C'MON.
LET ME INTRODUCE YOU TO -- MRS. ROSARIO!
GOOD AFTERNOON, MRS. ROSARIO!
ARE YOU ALSO GOING TO ISTANBUL?

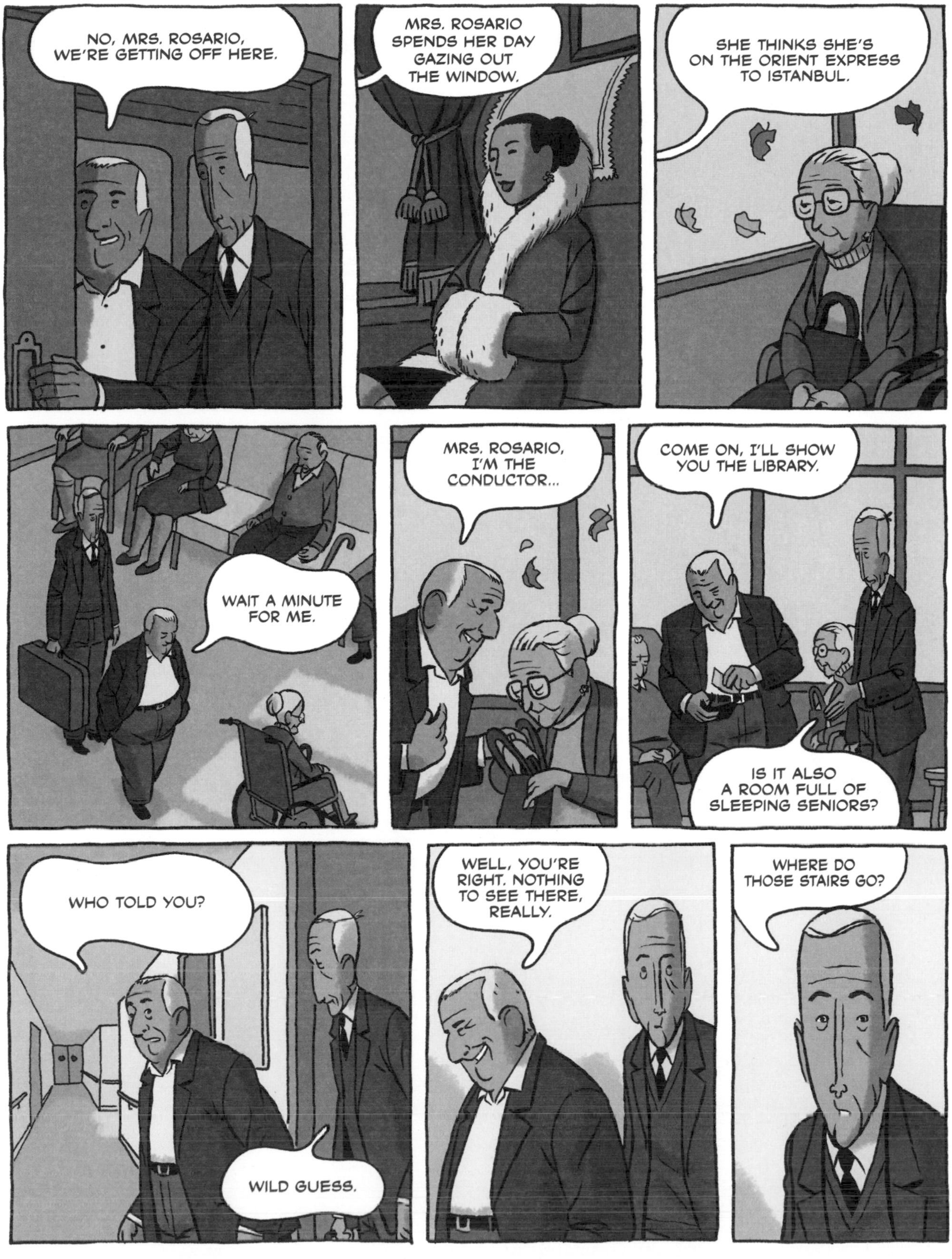
NO, MRS. ROSARIO, WE'RE GETTING OFF HERE.
MRS. ROSARIO SPENDS HER DAY GAZING OUT THE WINDOW.
SHE THINKS SHE'S ON THE ORIENT EXPRESS TO ISTANBUL.
WAIT A MINUTE FOR ME.
MRS. ROSARIO, I'M THE CONDUCTOR...
COME ON, I'LL SHOW YOU THE LIBRARY.
IS IT ALSO A ROOM FULL OF SLEEPING SENIORS?
WHO TOLD YOU?
WILD GUESS.
WELL, YOU'RE RIGHT. NOTHING TO SEE THERE, REALLY.
WHERE DO THOSE STAIRS GO?

THESE STAIRS?

WELL -- SEE, LIKE I SAID, THE HOME HAS TWO FLOORS. THE HEALTHY ONES -- THE COMPETENT -- LIVE ON OUR FLOOR. THE INCOMPETENT LIVE ON THE THE SECOND FLOOR.

THE INCOMPETENT?

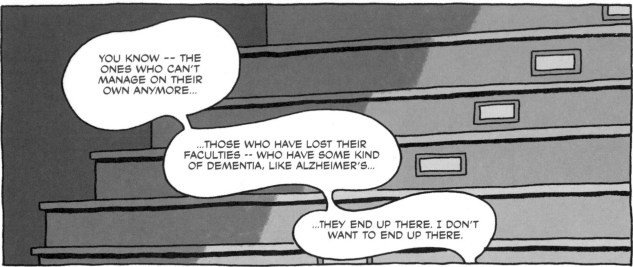

YOU KNOW -- THE ONES WHO CAN'T MANAGE ON THEIR OWN ANYMORE...

...THOSE WHO HAVE LOST THEIR FACULTIES -- WHO HAVE SOME KIND OF DEMENTIA, LIKE ALZHEIMER'S...

...THEY END UP THERE. I DON'T WANT TO END UP THERE.

I'D RATHER NOT GO UP. IT DEPRESSES ME.

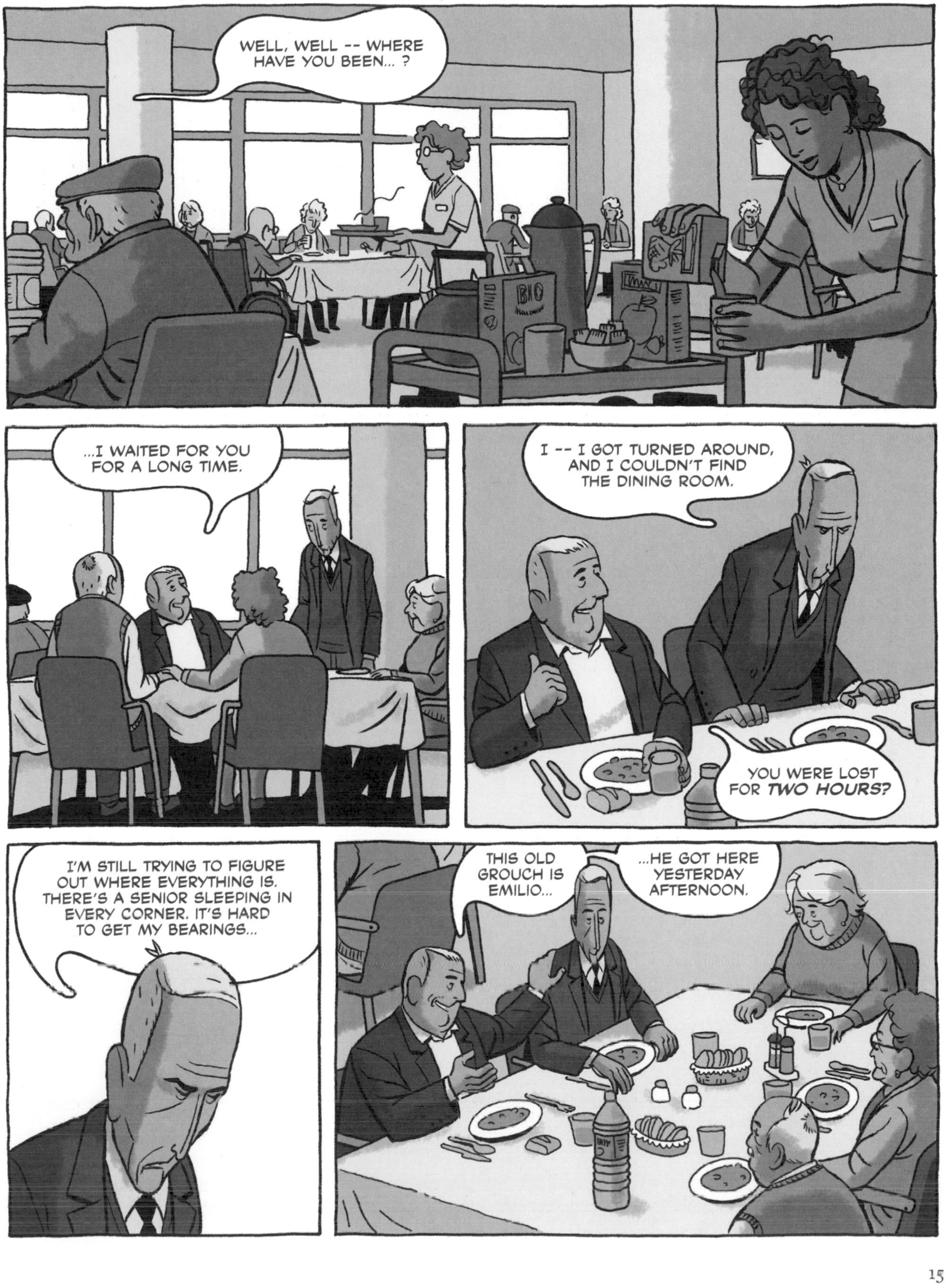

WELL, WELL -- WHERE HAVE YOU BEEN... ?
...I WAITED FOR YOU FOR A LONG TIME.
I -- I GOT TURNED AROUND, AND I COULDN'T FIND THE DINING ROOM.
YOU WERE LOST FOR TWO HOURS?
I'M STILL TRYING TO FIGURE OUT WHERE EVERYTHING IS. THERE'S A SENIOR SLEEPING IN EVERY CORNER. IT'S HARD TO GET MY BEARINGS...
THIS OLD GROUCH IS EMILIO...
...HE GOT HERE YESTERDAY AFTERNOON.

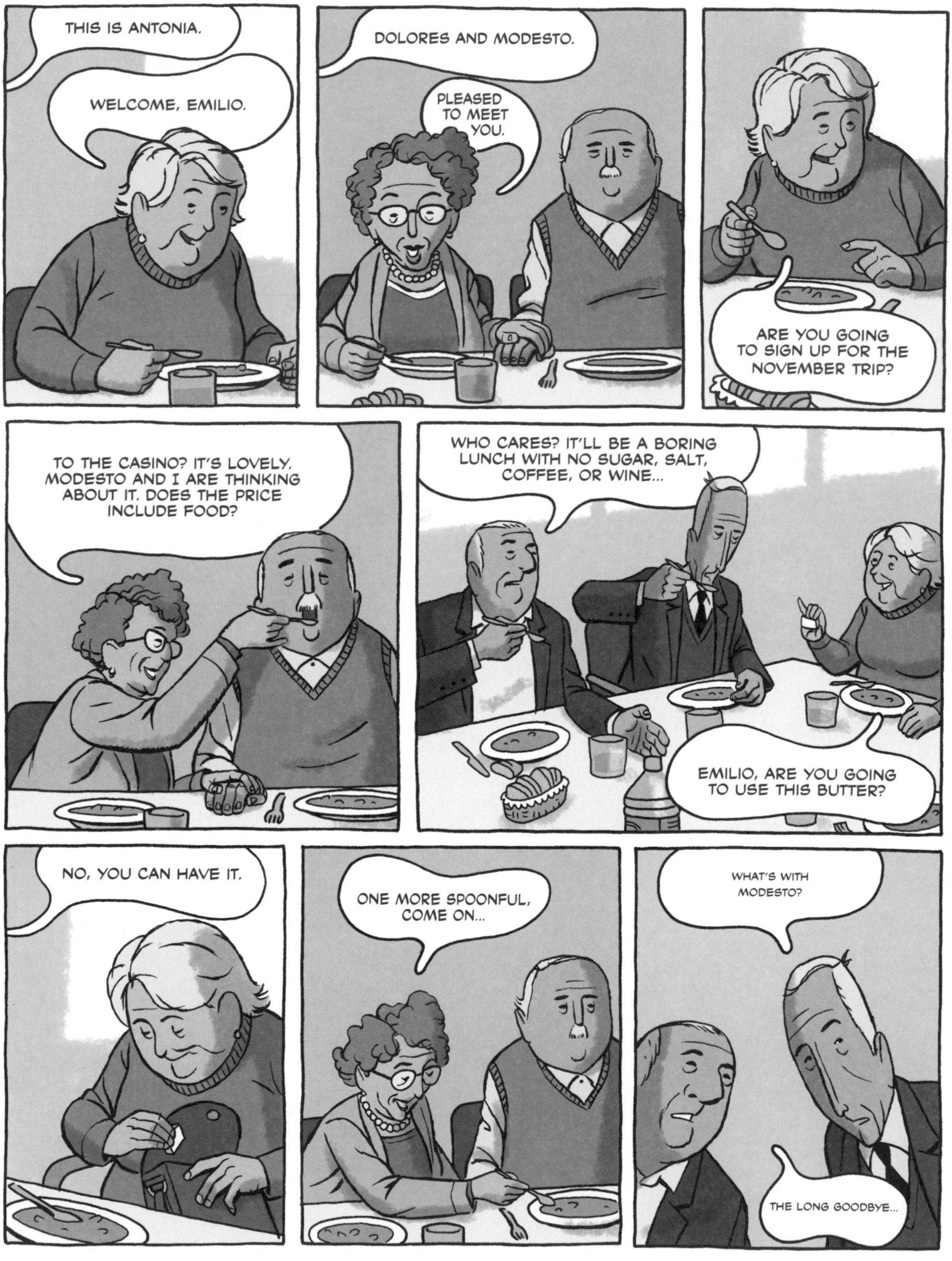
THIS IS ANTONIA.
WELCOME, EMILIO.
DOLORES AND MODESTO.
PLEASED TO MEET YOU.
ARE YOU GOING TO SIGN UP FOR THE NOVEMBER TRIP?
TO THE CASINO? IT'S LOVELY. MODESTO AND I ARE THINKING ABOUT IT. DOES THE PRICE INCLUDE FOOD?
WHO CARES? IT'LL BE A BORING LUNCH WITH NO SUGAR, SALT, COFFEE, OR WINE...
EMILIO, ARE YOU GOING TO USE THIS BUTTER?
NO, YOU CAN HAVE IT.
ONE MORE SPOONFUL, COME ON...
WHAT'S WITH MODESTO?
THE LONG GOODBYE...

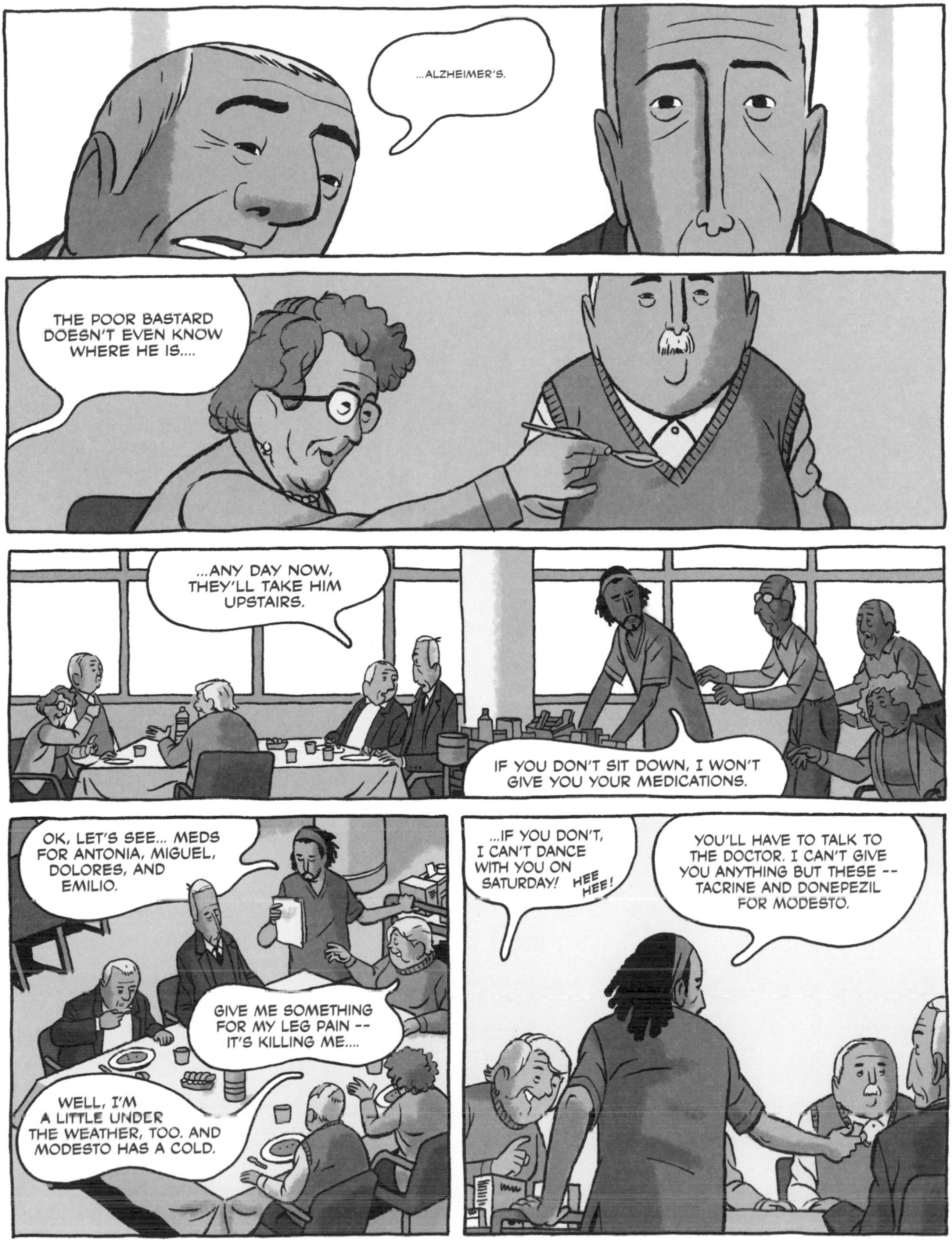
...ALZHEIMER'S.
THE POOR BASTARD DOESN'T EVEN KNOW WHERE HE IS....
...ANY DAY NOW, THEY'LL TAKE HIM UPSTAIRS.
IF YOU DON'T SIT DOWN, I WON'T GIVE YOU YOUR MEDICATIONS.
OK, LET'S SEE... MEDS FOR ANTONIA, MIGUEL, DOLORES, AND EMILIO.
GIVE ME SOMETHING FOR MY LEG PAIN -- IT'S KILLING ME....
WELL, I'M A LITTLE UNDER THE WEATHER, TOO. AND MODESTO HAS A COLD.
...IF YOU DON'T, I CAN'T DANCE WITH YOU ON SATURDAY!
HEE HEE!
YOU'LL HAVE TO TALK TO THE DOCTOR. I CAN'T GIVE YOU ANYTHING BUT THESE -- TACRINE AND DONEPEZIL FOR MODESTO.

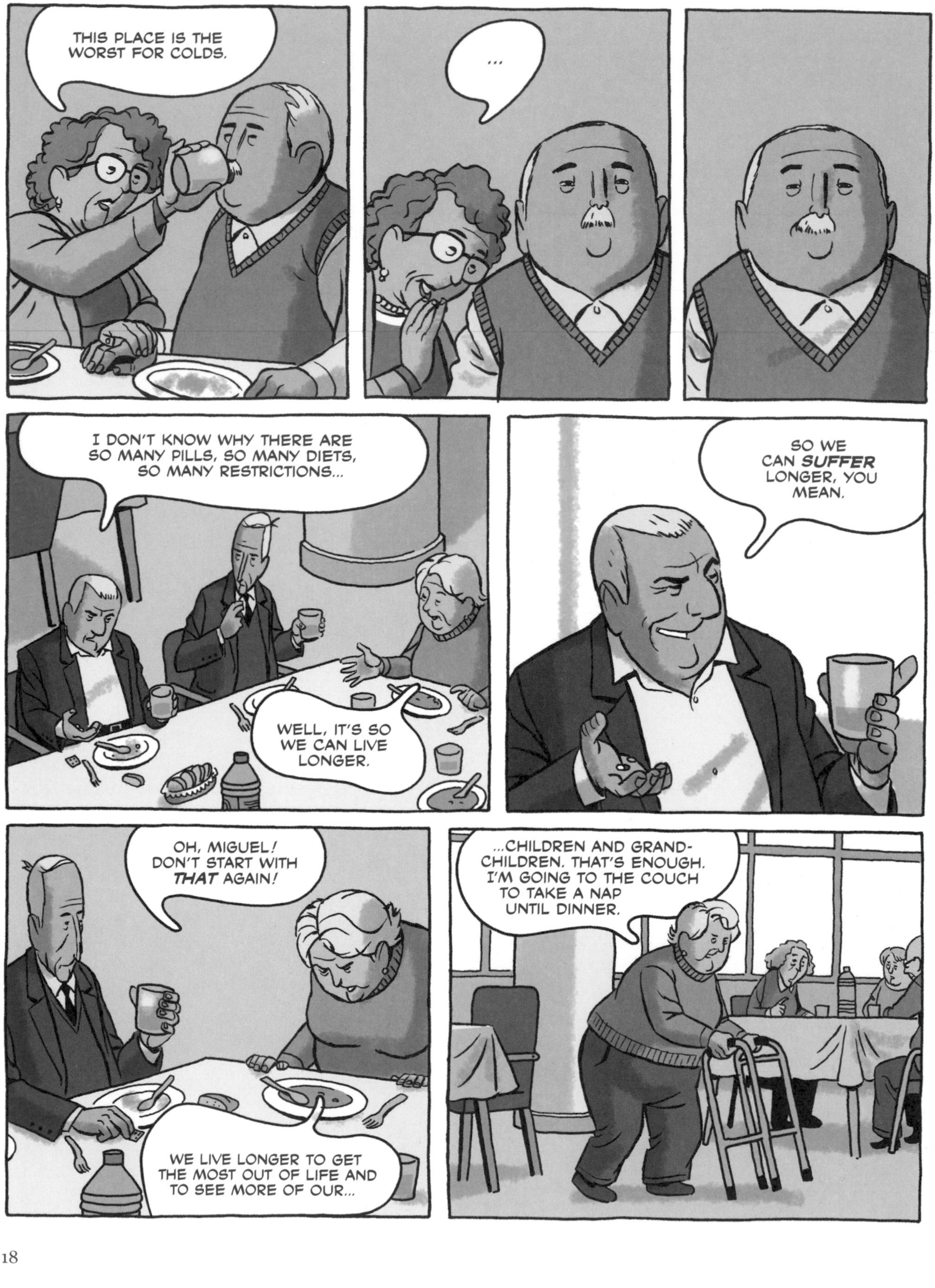
THIS PLACE IS THE WORST FOR COLDS.
...
I DON'T KNOW WHY THERE ARE SO MANY PILLS, SO MANY DIETS, SO MANY RESTRICTIONS...
WELL, IT'S SO WE CAN LIVE LONGER.
SO WE CAN *SUFFER* LONGER, YOU MEAN.
OH, MIGUEL! DON'T START WITH *THAT* AGAIN!
WE LIVE LONGER TO GET THE MOST OUT OF LIFE AND TO SEE MORE OF OUR...
...CHILDREN AND GRAND-CHILDREN. THAT'S ENOUGH. I'M GOING TO THE COUCH TO TAKE A NAP UNTIL DINNER.

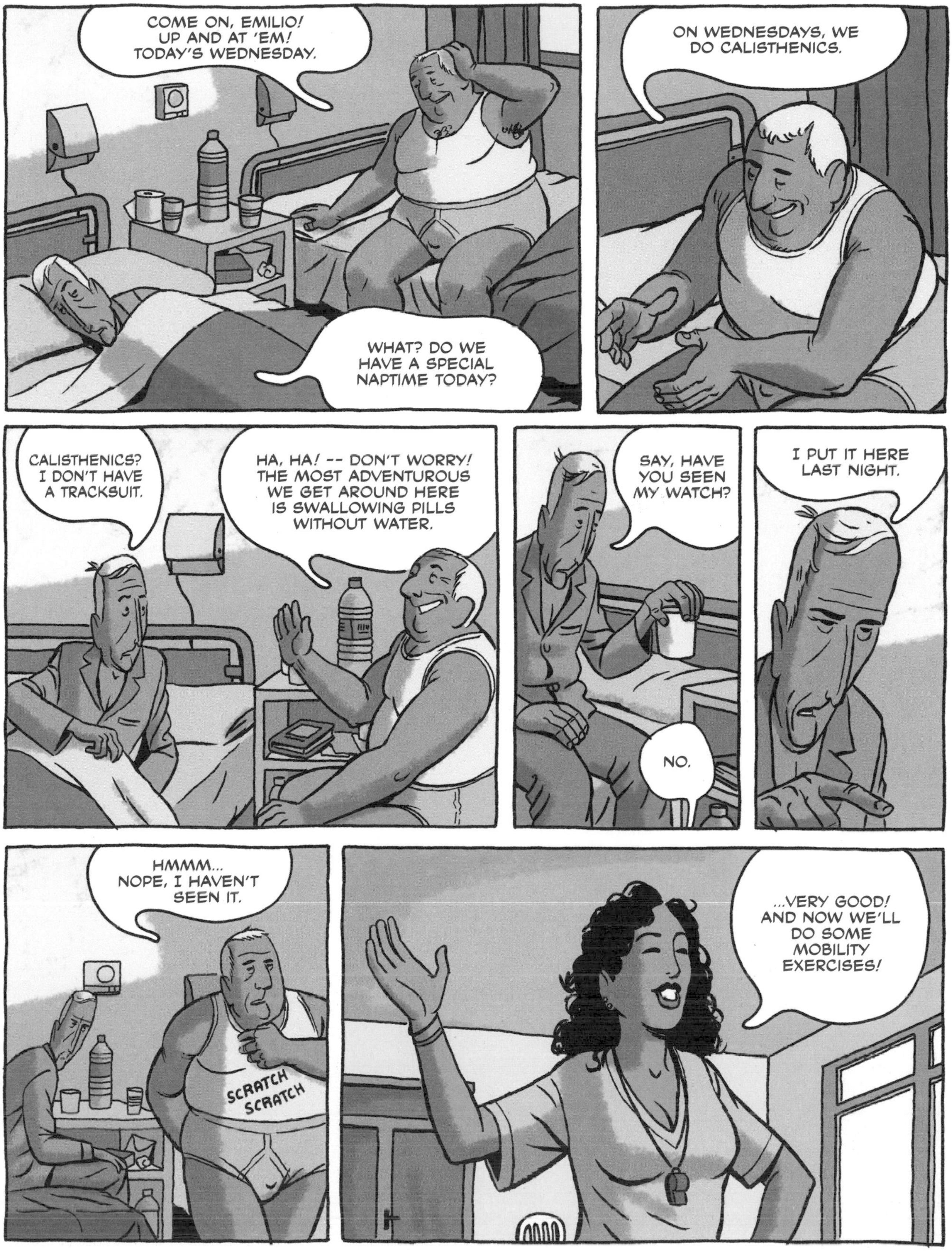
COME ON, EMILIO! UP AND AT 'EM! TODAY'S WEDNESDAY.
WHAT? DO WE HAVE A SPECIAL NAPTIME TODAY?
ON WEDNESDAYS, WE DO CALISTHENICS.
CALISTHENICS? I DON'T HAVE A TRACKSUIT.
HA, HA! -- DON'T WORRY! THE MOST ADVENTUROUS WE GET AROUND HERE IS SWALLOWING PILLS WITHOUT WATER.
SAY, HAVE YOU SEEN MY WATCH?
NO.
I PUT IT HERE LAST NIGHT.
HMMM... NOPE, I HAVEN'T SEEN IT.
SCRATCH SCRATCH
...VERY GOOD! AND NOW WE'LL DO SOME MOBILITY EXERCISES!

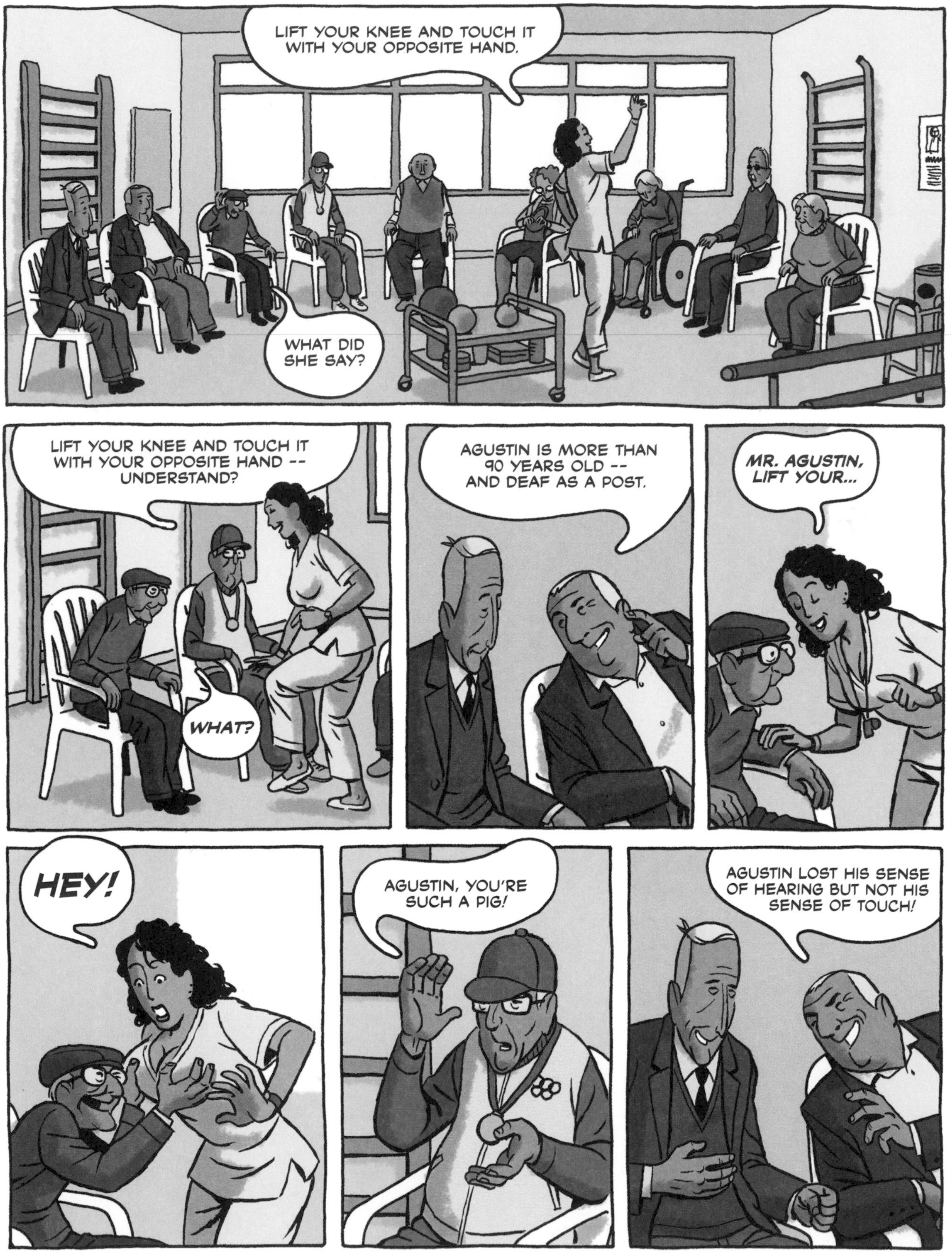
LIFT YOUR KNEE AND TOUCH IT WITH YOUR OPPOSITE HAND.
WHAT DID SHE SAY?
LIFT YOUR KNEE AND TOUCH IT WITH YOUR OPPOSITE HAND -- UNDERSTAND?
WHAT?
AGUSTIN IS MORE THAN 90 YEARS OLD -- AND DEAF AS A POST.
MR. AGUSTIN, LIFT YOUR...
HEY!
AGUSTIN, YOU'RE SUCH A PIG!
AGUSTIN LOST HIS SENSE OF HEARING BUT NOT HIS SENSE OF TOUCH!

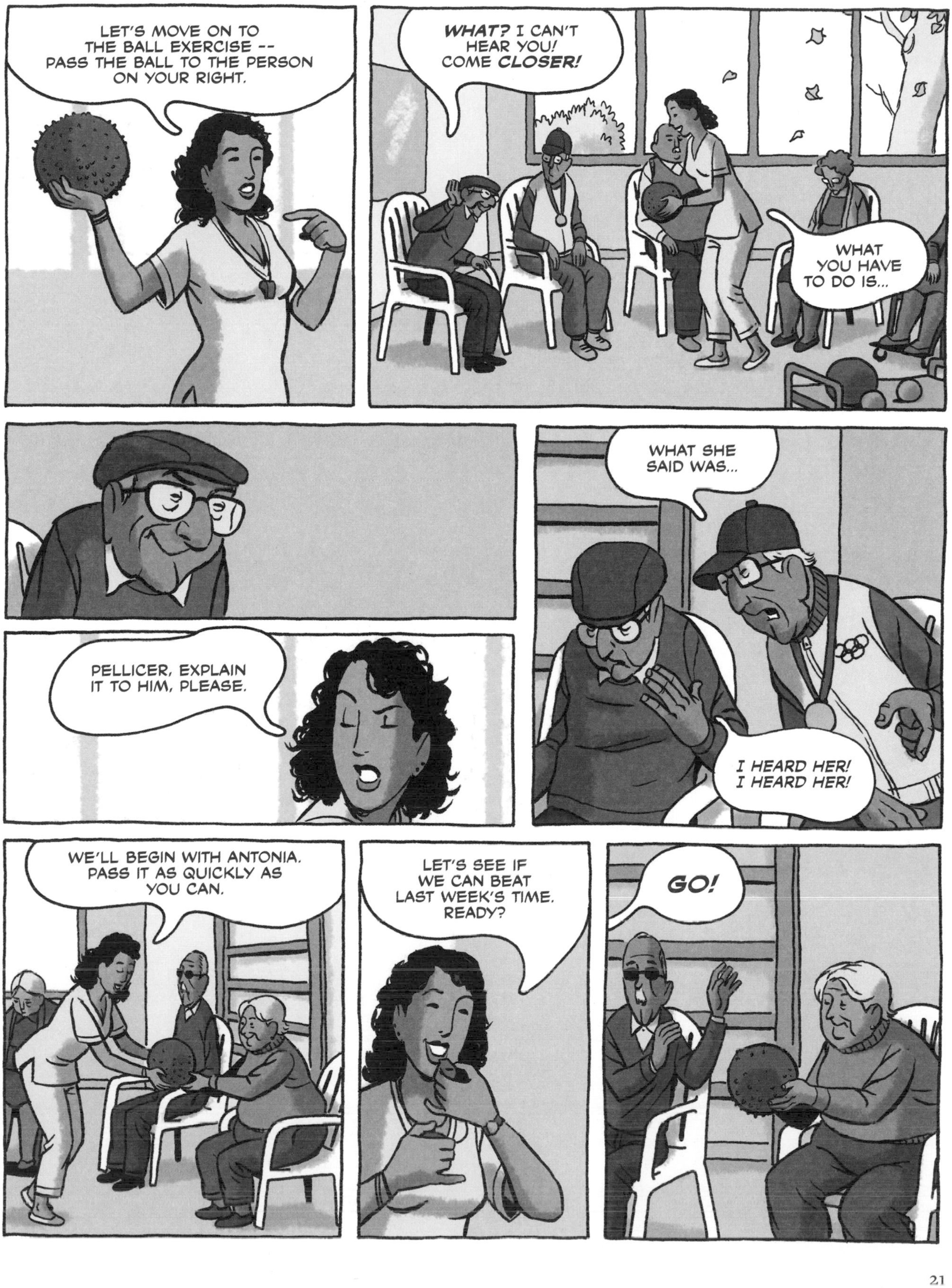
LET'S MOVE ON TO THE BALL EXERCISE -- PASS THE BALL TO THE PERSON ON YOUR RIGHT.
WHAT? I CAN'T HEAR YOU! COME CLOSER!
WHAT YOU HAVE TO DO IS...
WHAT SHE SAID WAS...
PELLICER, EXPLAIN IT TO HIM, PLEASE.
I HEARD HER! I HEARD HER!
WE'LL BEGIN WITH ANTONIA. PASS IT AS QUICKLY AS YOU CAN.
LET'S SEE IF WE CAN BEAT LAST WEEK'S TIME. READY?
GO!

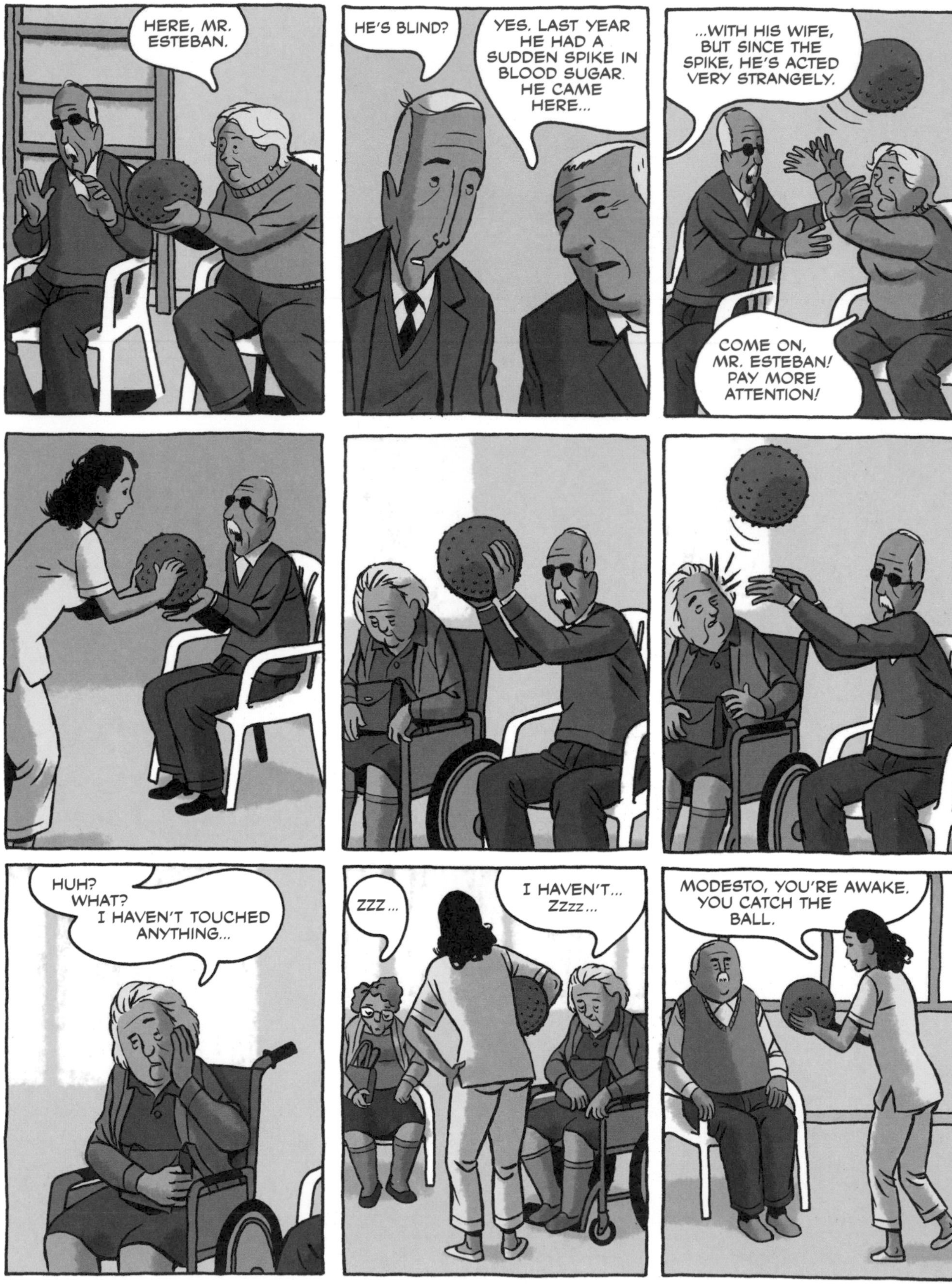
HERE, MR. ESTEBAN.
HE'S BLIND?
YES. LAST YEAR HE HAD A SUDDEN SPIKE IN BLOOD SUGAR. HE CAME HERE...
...WITH HIS WIFE, BUT SINCE THE SPIKE, HE'S ACTED VERY STRANGELY.
COME ON, MR. ESTEBAN! PAY MORE ATTENTION!
HUH? WHAT? I HAVEN'T TOUCHED ANYTHING...
ZZZ...
I HAVEN'T... ZZzz...
MODESTO, YOU'RE AWAKE. YOU CATCH THE BALL.

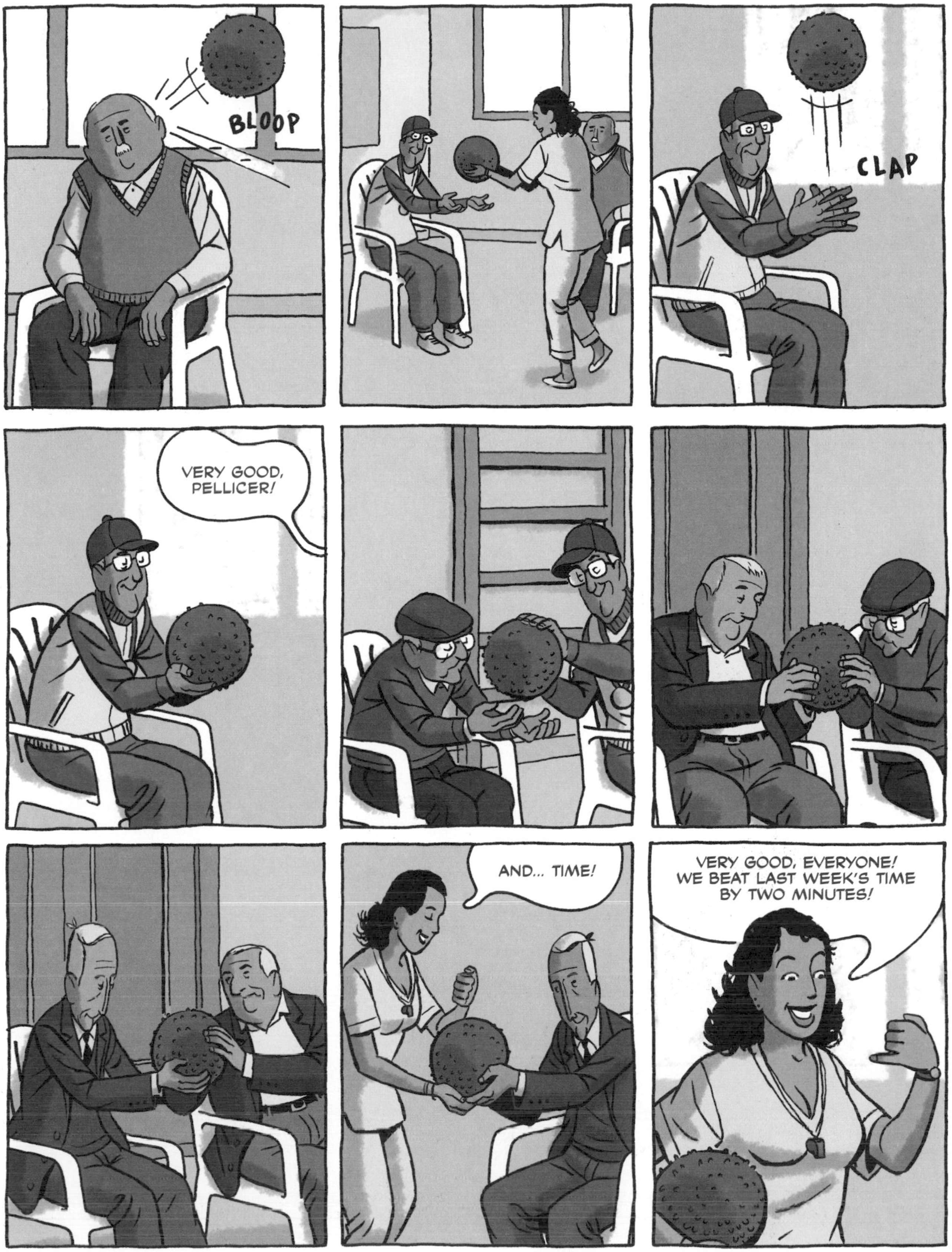
BLOOP
CLAP
VERY GOOD, PELLICER!
AND... TIME!
VERY GOOD, EVERYONE! WE BEAT LAST WEEK'S TIME BY TWO MINUTES!

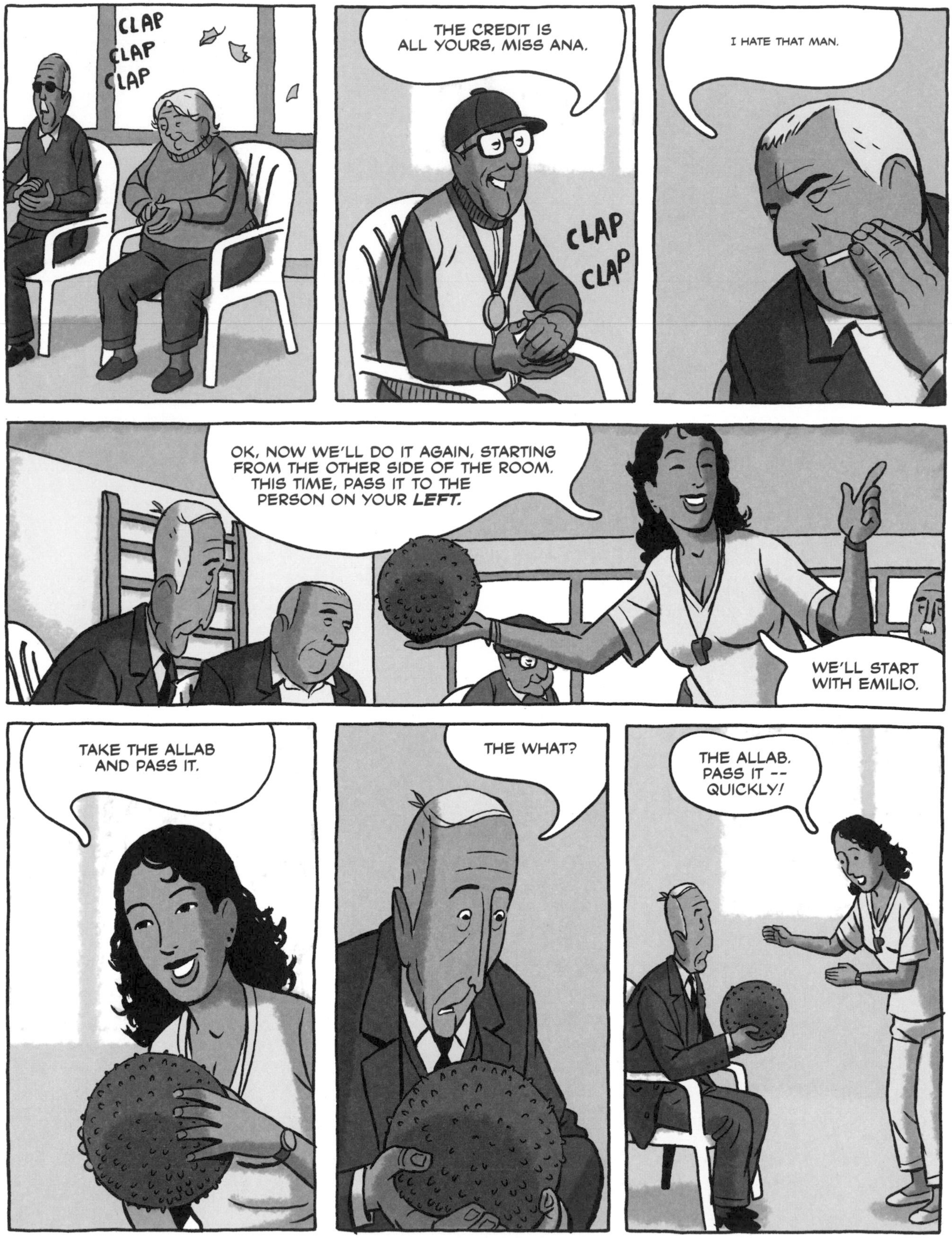
CLAP
CLAP
CLAP
THE CREDIT IS ALL YOURS, MISS ANA.
CLAP
CLAP
I HATE THAT MAN.
OK, NOW WE'LL DO IT AGAIN, STARTING FROM THE OTHER SIDE OF THE ROOM. THIS TIME, PASS IT TO THE PERSON ON YOUR LEFT.
WE'LL START WITH EMILIO.
TAKE THE ALLAB AND PASS IT.
THE WHAT?
THE ALLAB. PASS IT -- QUICKLY!

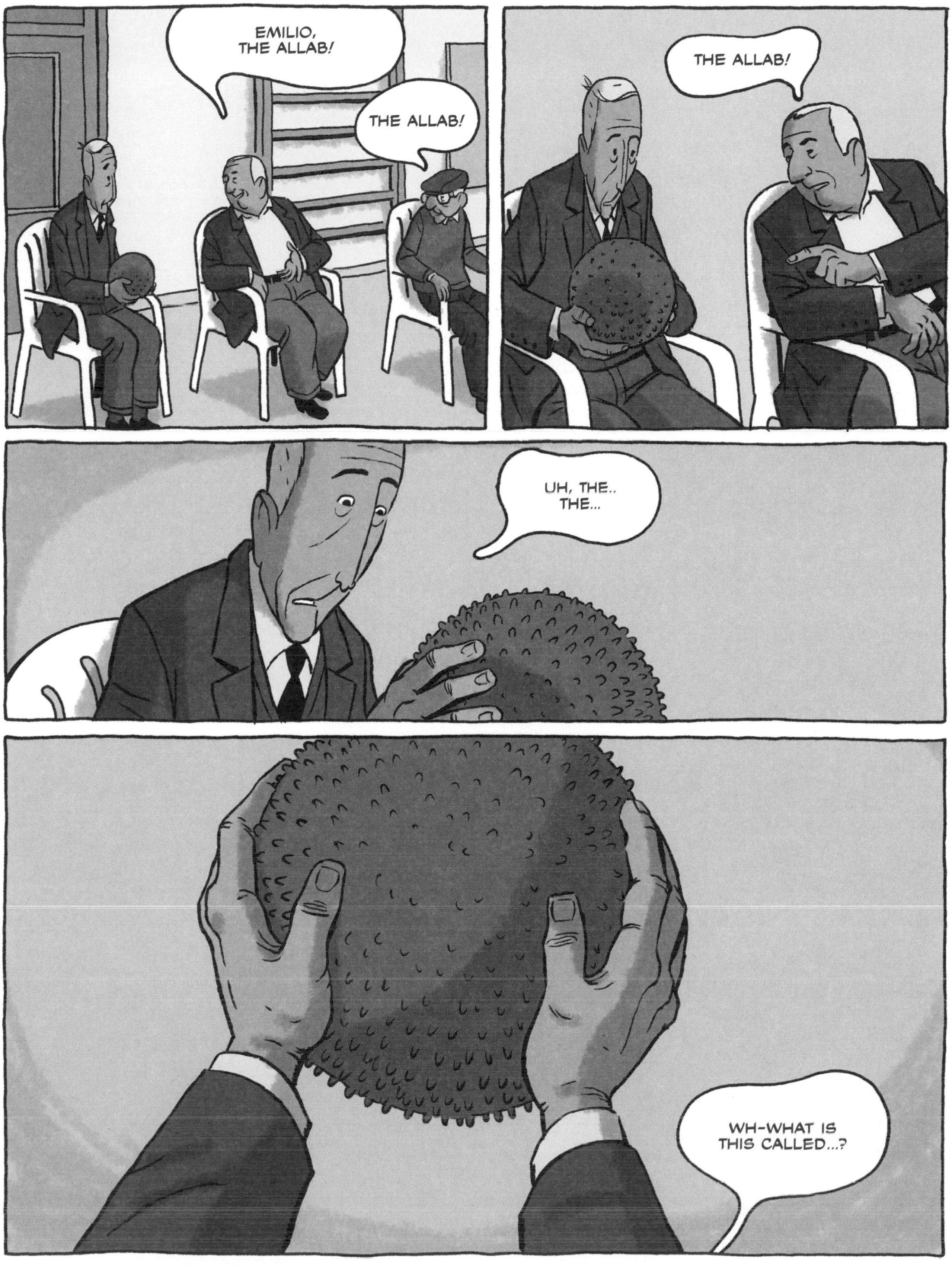
EMILIO, THE ALLAB!
THE ALLAB!
THE ALLAB!
UH, THE.. THE...
WH-WHAT IS THIS CALLED...?

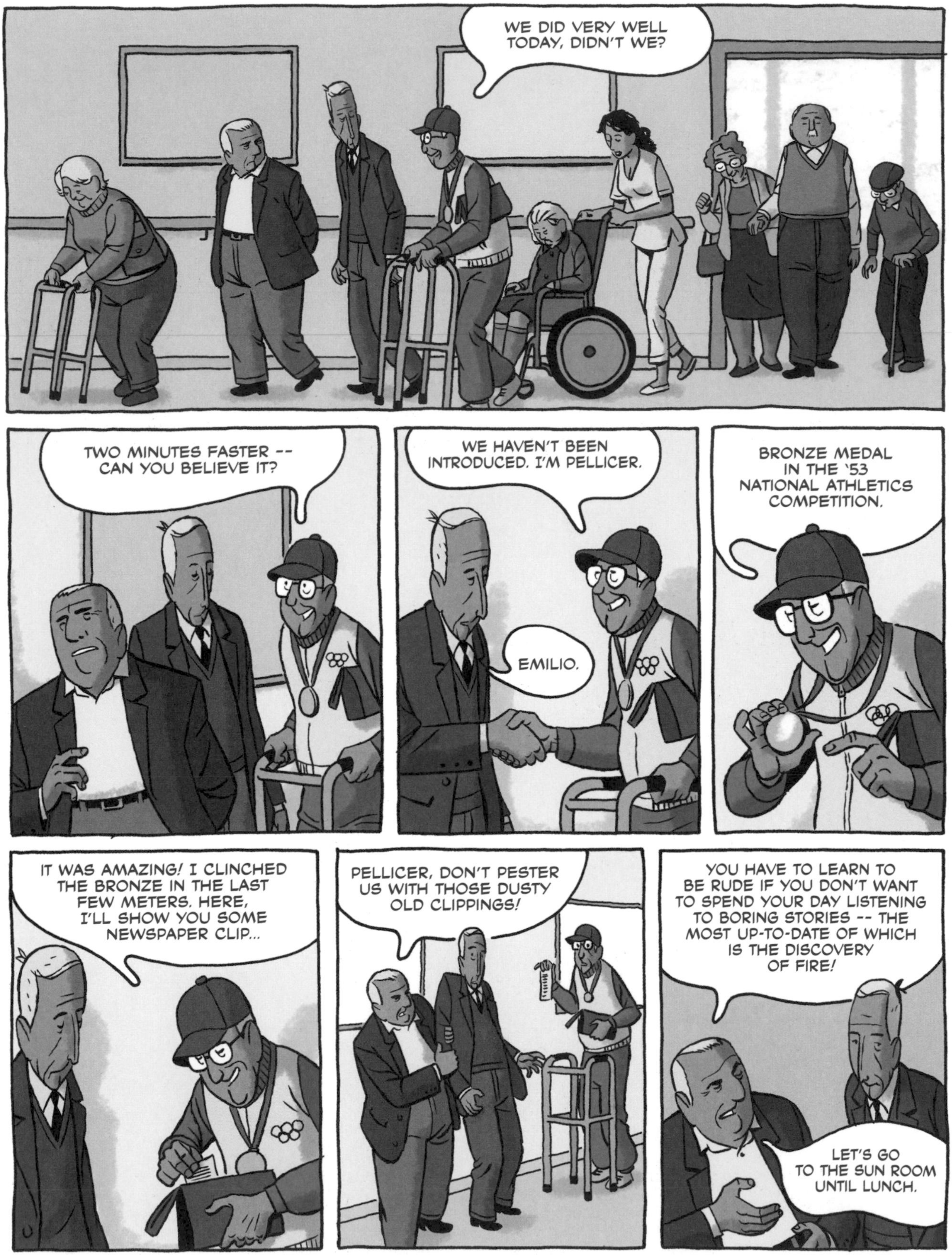
WE DID VERY WELL TODAY, DIDN'T WE?
TWO MINUTES FASTER -- CAN YOU BELIEVE IT?
WE HAVEN'T BEEN INTRODUCED. I'M PELLICER.
EMILIO.
BRONZE MEDAL IN THE '53 NATIONAL ATHLETICS COMPETITION.
IT WAS AMAZING! I CLINCHED THE BRONZE IN THE LAST FEW METERS. HERE, I'LL SHOW YOU SOME NEWSPAPER CLIP...
PELLICER, DON'T PESTER US WITH THOSE DUSTY OLD CLIPPINGS!
YOU HAVE TO LEARN TO BE RUDE IF YOU DON'T WANT TO SPEND YOUR DAY LISTENING TO BORING STORIES -- THE MOST UP-TO-DATE OF WHICH IS THE DISCOVERY OF FIRE!
LET'S GO TO THE SUN ROOM UNTIL LUNCH.

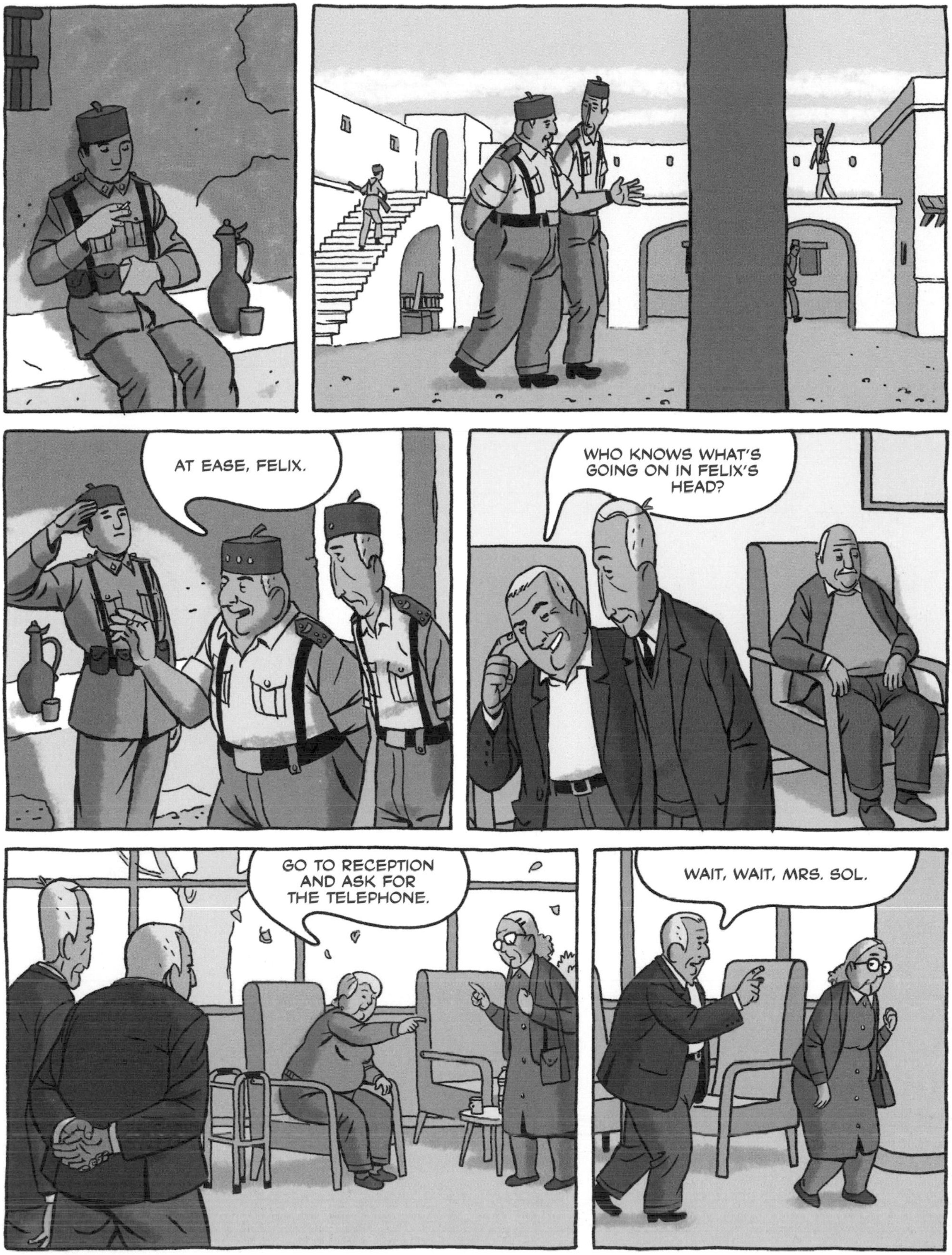
AT EASE, FELIX.
WHO KNOWS WHAT'S GOING ON IN FELIX'S HEAD?
GO TO RECEPTION AND ASK FOR THE TELEPHONE.
WAIT, WAIT, MRS. SOL.

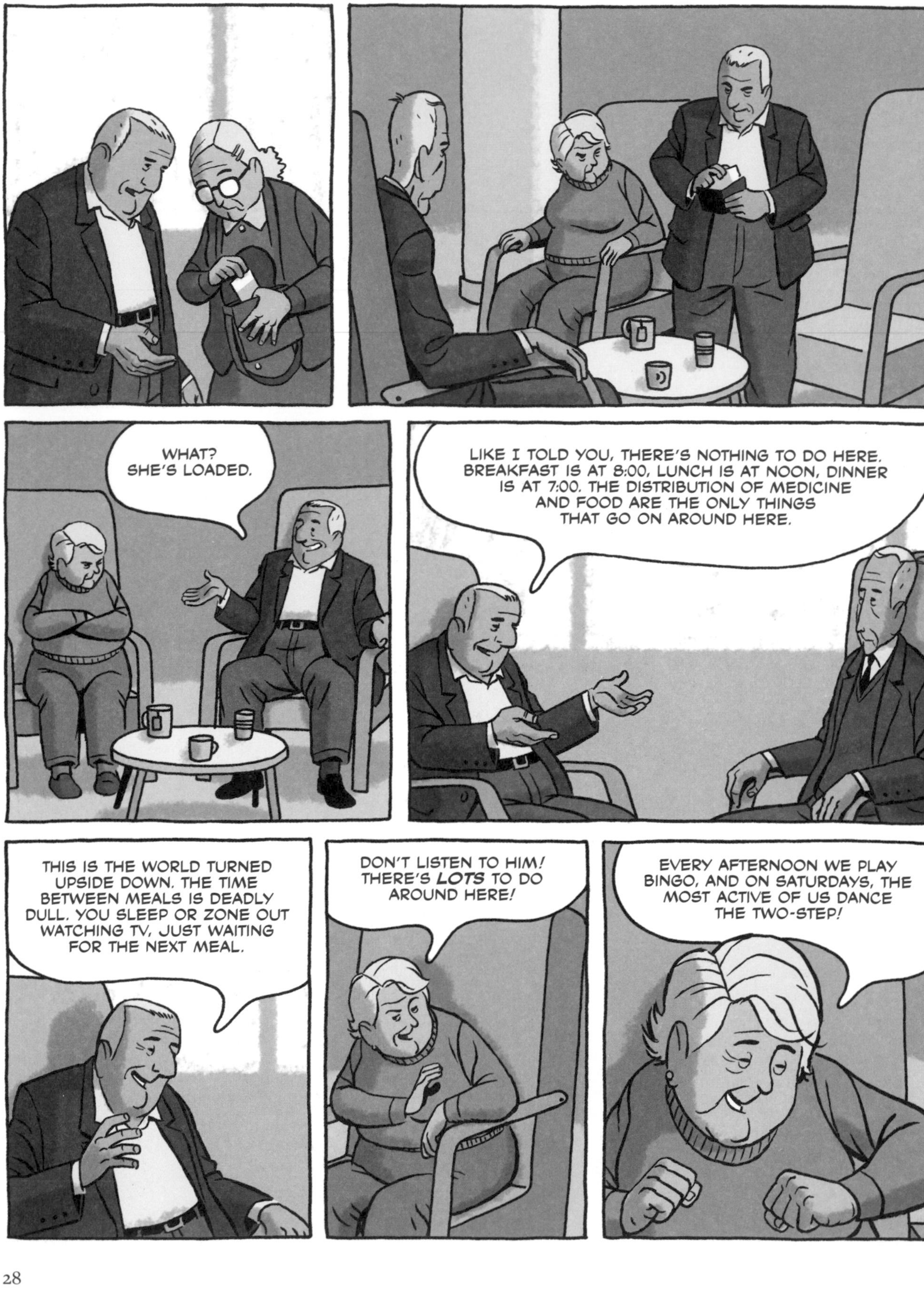
WHAT? SHE'S LOADED.
LIKE I TOLD YOU, THERE'S NOTHING TO DO HERE. BREAKFAST IS AT 8:00, LUNCH IS AT NOON, DINNER IS AT 7:00. THE DISTRIBUTION OF MEDICINE AND FOOD ARE THE ONLY THINGS THAT GO ON AROUND HERE.
THIS IS THE WORLD TURNED UPSIDE DOWN. THE TIME BETWEEN MEALS IS DEADLY DULL. YOU SLEEP OR ZONE OUT WATCHING TV, JUST WAITING FOR THE NEXT MEAL.
DON'T LISTEN TO HIM! THERE'S *LOTS* TO DO AROUND HERE!
EVERY AFTERNOON WE PLAY BINGO, AND ON SATURDAYS, THE MOST ACTIVE OF US DANCE THE TWO-STEP!

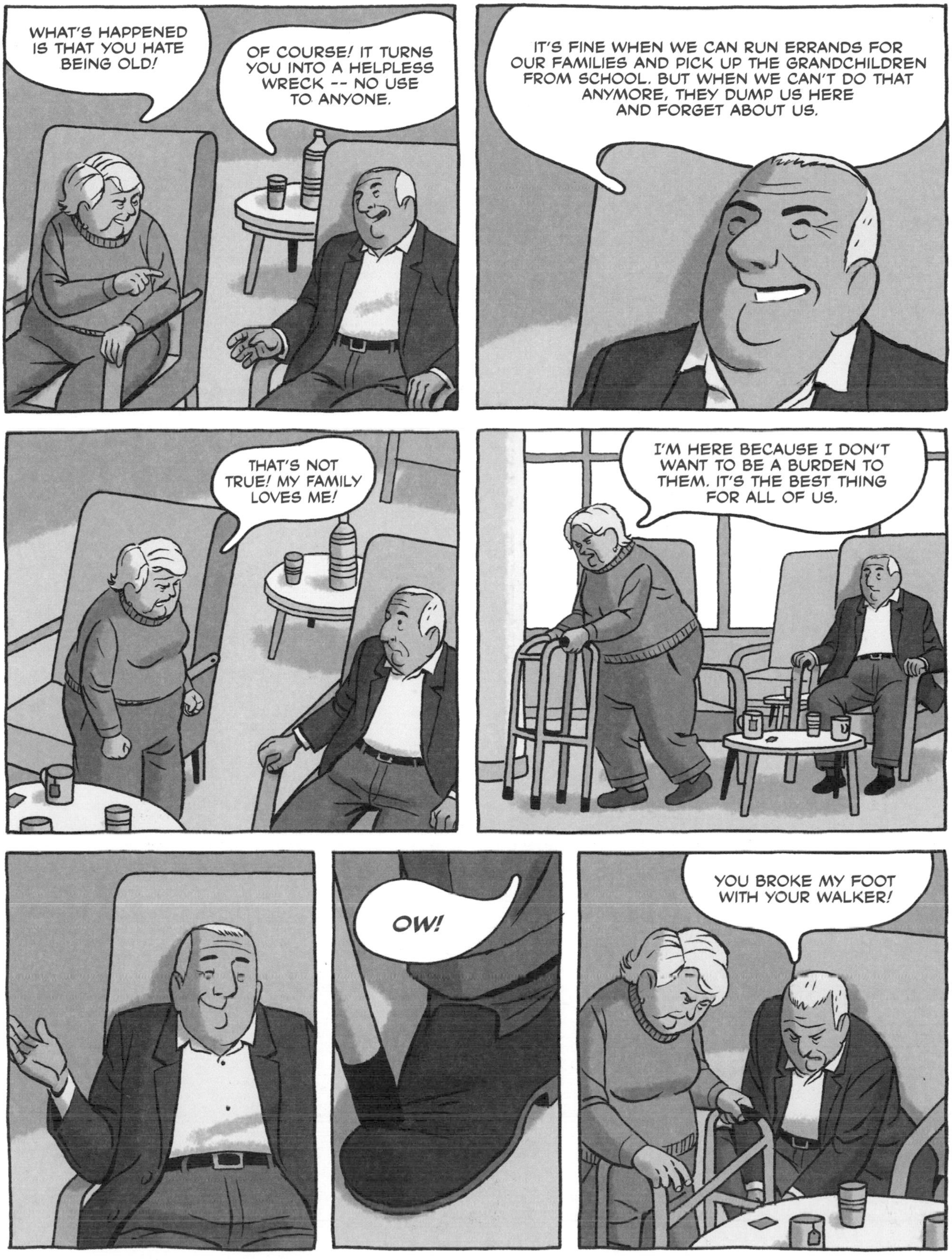
WHAT'S HAPPENED IS THAT YOU HATE BEING OLD!
OF COURSE! IT TURNS YOU INTO A HELPLESS WRECK -- NO USE TO ANYONE.
IT'S FINE WHEN WE CAN RUN ERRANDS FOR OUR FAMILIES AND PICK UP THE GRANDCHILDREN FROM SCHOOL. BUT WHEN WE CAN'T DO THAT ANYMORE, THEY DUMP US HERE AND FORGET ABOUT US.
THAT'S NOT TRUE! MY FAMILY LOVES ME!
I'M HERE BECAUSE I DON'T WANT TO BE A BURDEN TO THEM. IT'S THE BEST THING FOR ALL OF US.
OW!
YOU BROKE MY FOOT WITH YOUR WALKER!

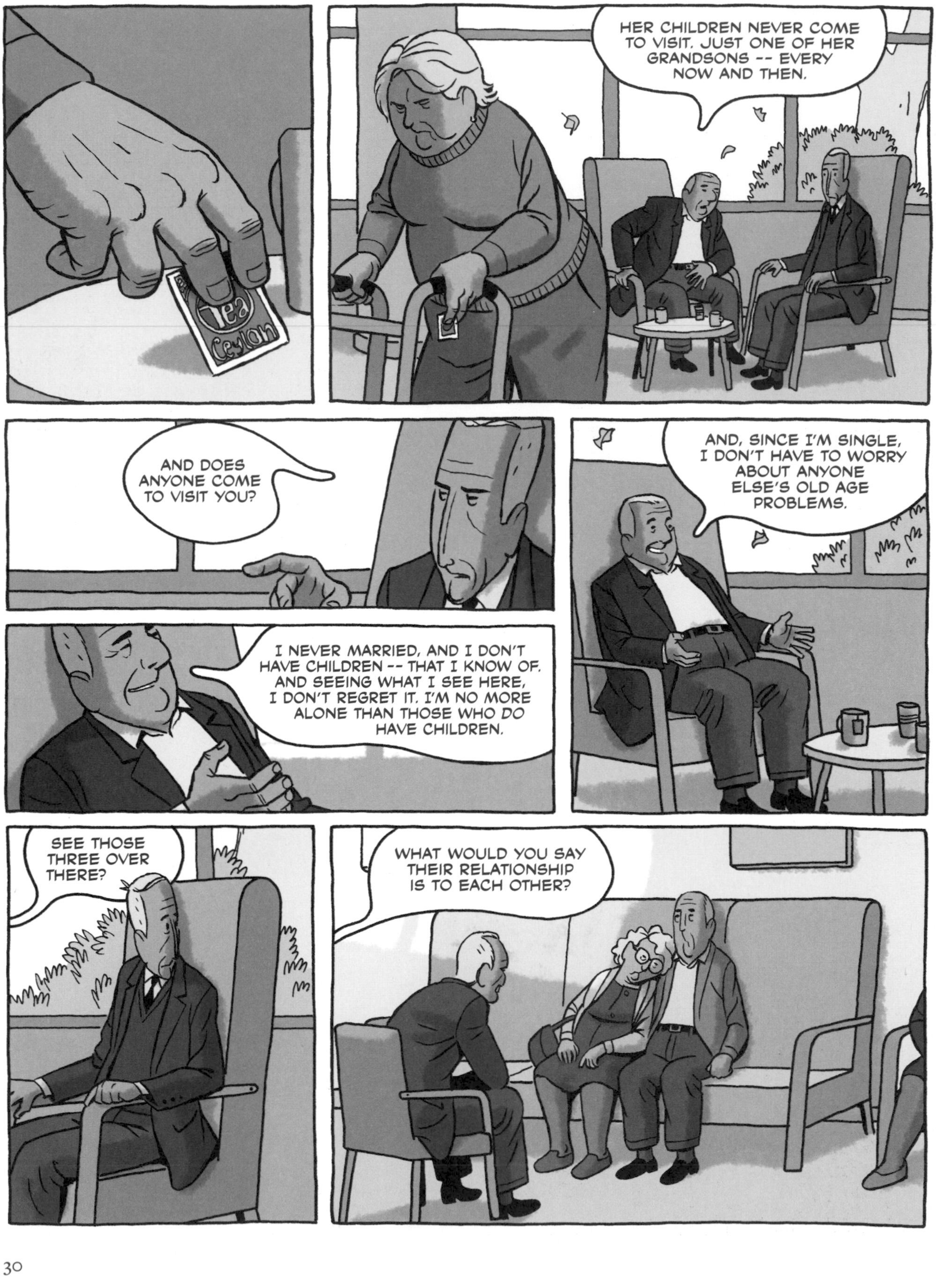
Tea Ceylon
HER CHILDREN NEVER COME TO VISIT. JUST ONE OF HER GRANDSONS -- EVERY NOW AND THEN.
AND DOES ANYONE COME TO VISIT YOU?
I NEVER MARRIED, AND I DON'T HAVE CHILDREN -- THAT I KNOW OF. AND SEEING WHAT I SEE HERE, I DON'T REGRET IT. I'M NO MORE ALONE THAN THOSE WHO *DO* HAVE CHILDREN.
AND, SINCE I'M SINGLE, I DON'T HAVE TO WORRY ABOUT ANYONE ELSE'S OLD AGE PROBLEMS.
SEE THOSE THREE OVER THERE?
WHAT WOULD YOU SAY THEIR RELATIONSHIP IS TO EACH OTHER?

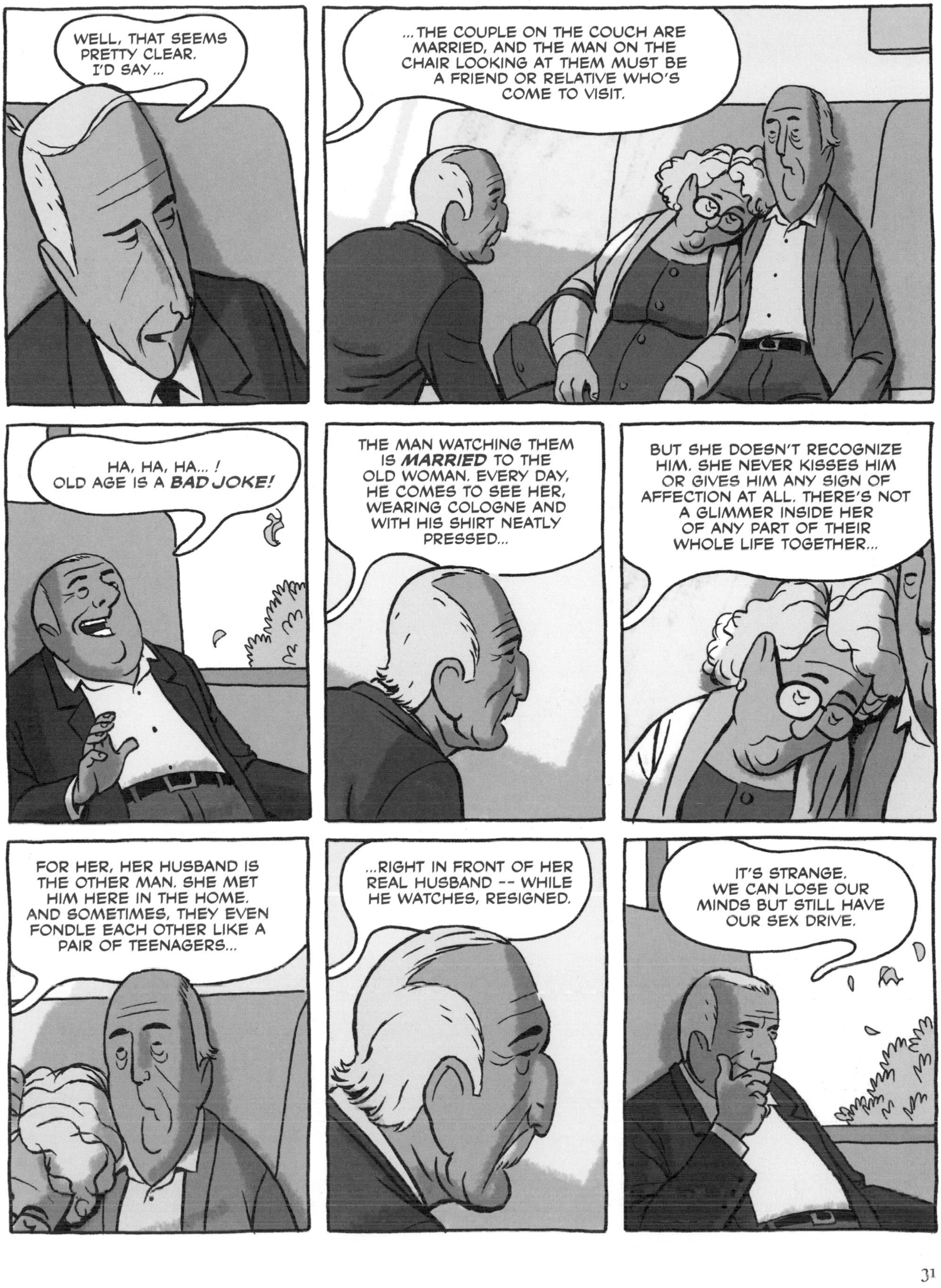
WELL, THAT SEEMS PRETTY CLEAR. I'D SAY...
...THE COUPLE ON THE COUCH ARE MARRIED, AND THE MAN ON THE CHAIR LOOKING AT THEM MUST BE A FRIEND OR RELATIVE WHO'S COME TO VISIT.
HA, HA, HA... ! OLD AGE IS A ***BAD JOKE!***
THE MAN WATCHING THEM IS ***MARRIED*** TO THE OLD WOMAN. EVERY DAY, HE COMES TO SEE HER, WEARING COLOGNE AND WITH HIS SHIRT NEATLY PRESSED...
BUT SHE DOESN'T RECOGNIZE HIM. SHE NEVER KISSES HIM OR GIVES HIM ANY SIGN OF AFFECTION AT ALL. THERE'S NOT A GLIMMER INSIDE HER OF ANY PART OF THEIR WHOLE LIFE TOGETHER...
FOR HER, HER HUSBAND IS THE OTHER MAN. SHE MET HIM HERE IN THE HOME. AND SOMETIMES, THEY EVEN FONDLE EACH OTHER LIKE A PAIR OF TEENAGERS...
...RIGHT IN FRONT OF HER REAL HUSBAND -- WHILE HE WATCHES, RESIGNED.
IT'S STRANGE. WE CAN LOSE OUR MINDS BUT STILL HAVE OUR SEX DRIVE.

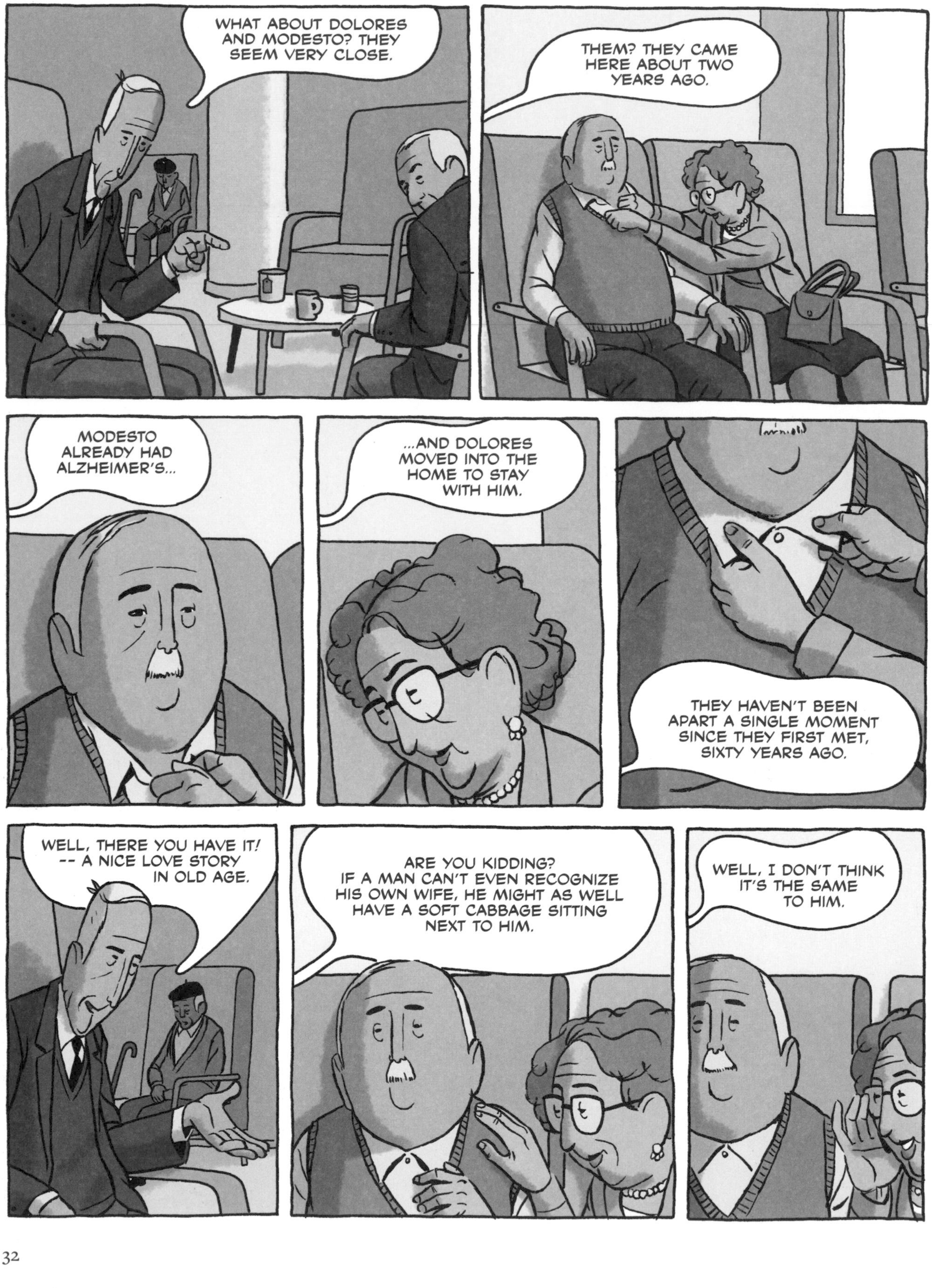
WHAT ABOUT DOLORES AND MODESTO? THEY SEEM VERY CLOSE.
THEM? THEY CAME HERE ABOUT TWO YEARS AGO.
MODESTO ALREADY HAD ALZHEIMER'S...
...AND DOLORES MOVED INTO THE HOME TO STAY WITH HIM.
THEY HAVEN'T BEEN APART A SINGLE MOMENT SINCE THEY FIRST MET, SIXTY YEARS AGO.
WELL, THERE YOU HAVE IT! -- A NICE LOVE STORY IN OLD AGE.
ARE YOU KIDDING? IF A MAN CAN'T EVEN RECOGNIZE HIS OWN WIFE, HE MIGHT AS WELL HAVE A SOFT CABBAGE SITTING NEXT TO HIM.
WELL, I DON'T THINK IT'S THE SAME TO HIM.

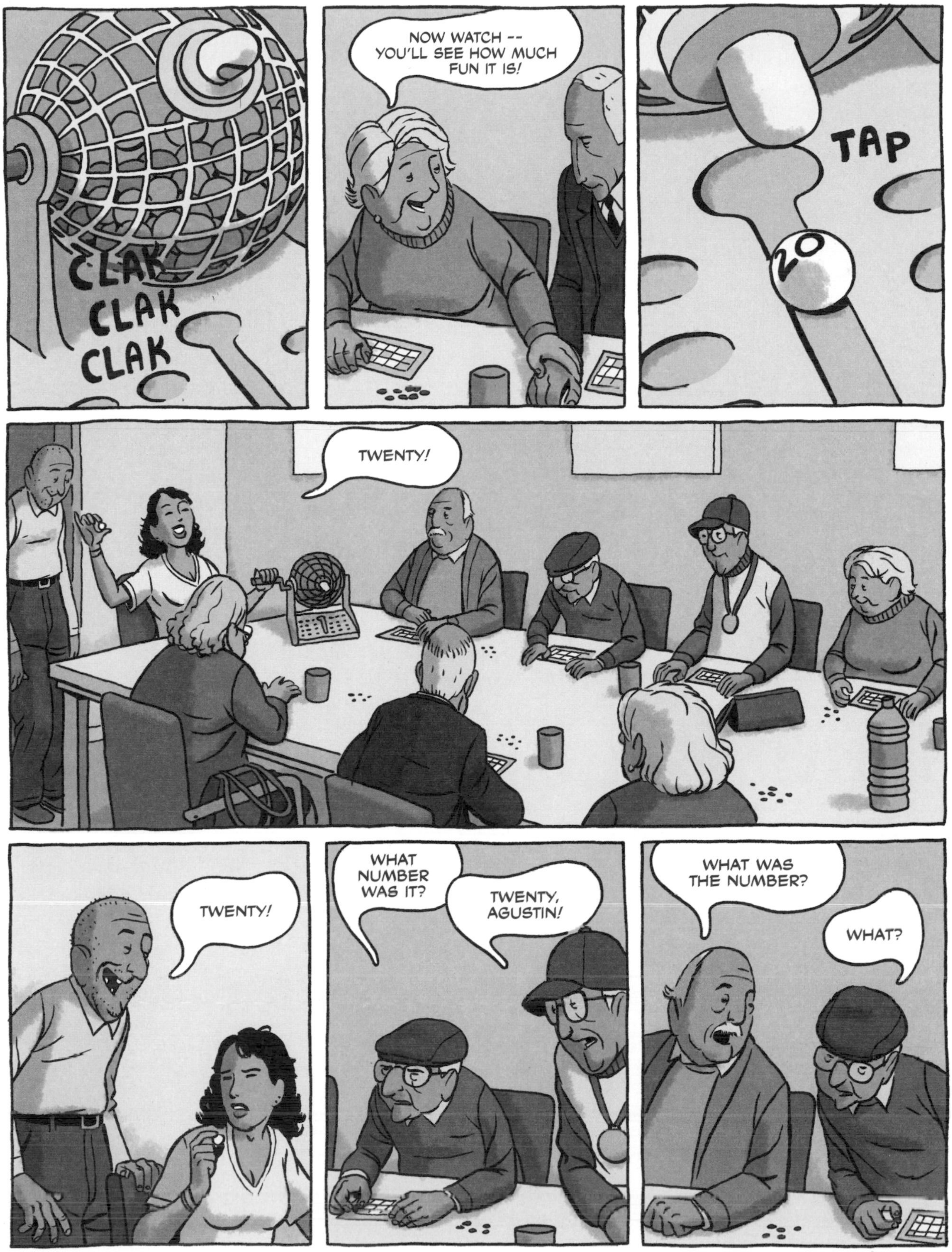
CLAK
CLAK
CLAK
NOW WATCH -- YOU'LL SEE HOW MUCH FUN IT IS!
TAP
20
TWENTY!
TWENTY!
WHAT NUMBER WAS IT?
TWENTY, AGUSTIN!
WHAT WAS THE NUMBER?
WHAT?

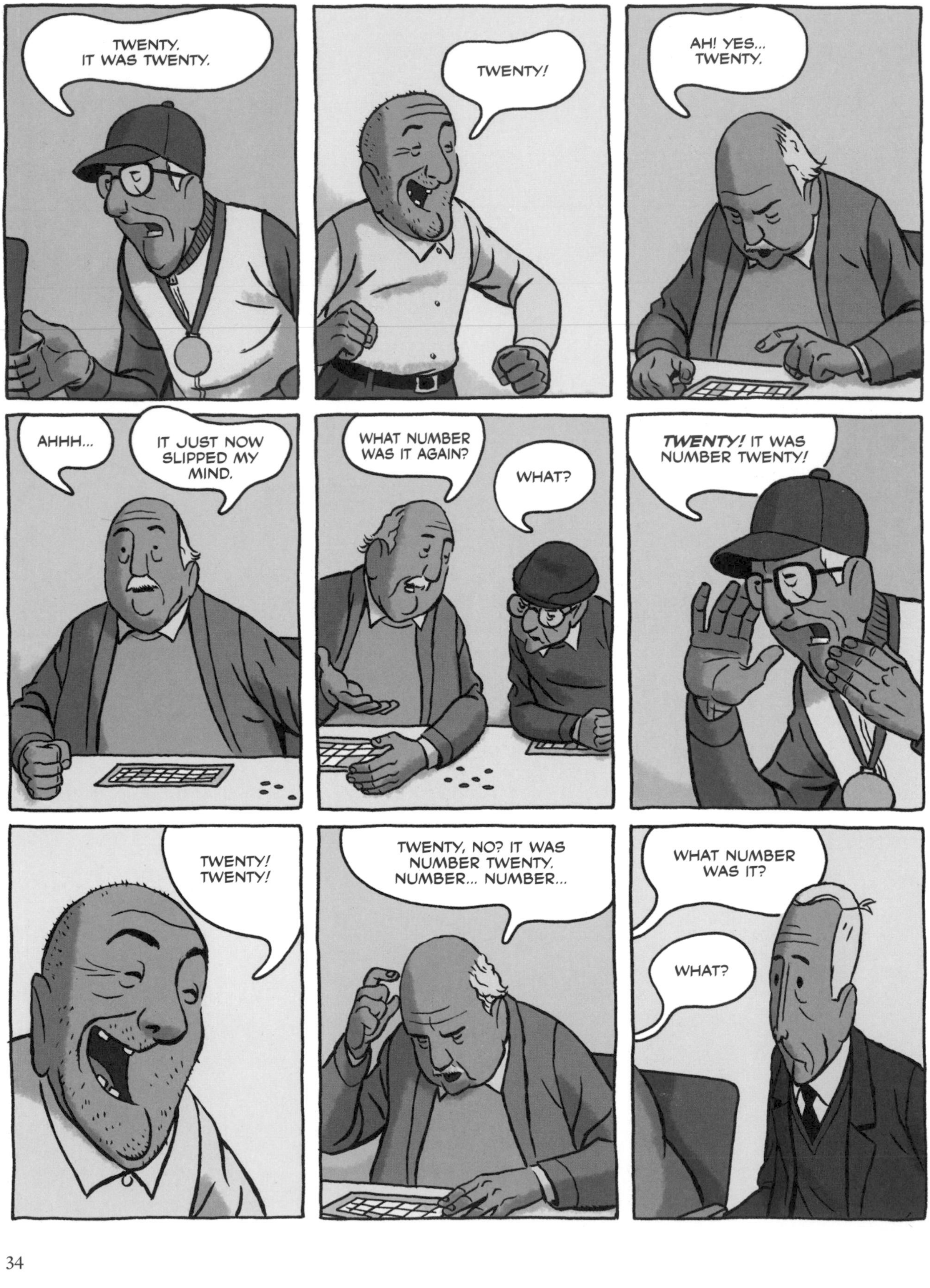
TWENTY. IT WAS TWENTY.
TWENTY!
AH! YES... TWENTY.
AHHH...
IT JUST NOW SLIPPED MY MIND.
WHAT NUMBER WAS IT AGAIN?
WHAT?
TWENTY! IT WAS NUMBER TWENTY!
TWENTY! TWENTY!
TWENTY, NO? IT WAS NUMBER TWENTY. NUMBER... NUMBER...
WHAT NUMBER WAS IT?
WHAT?

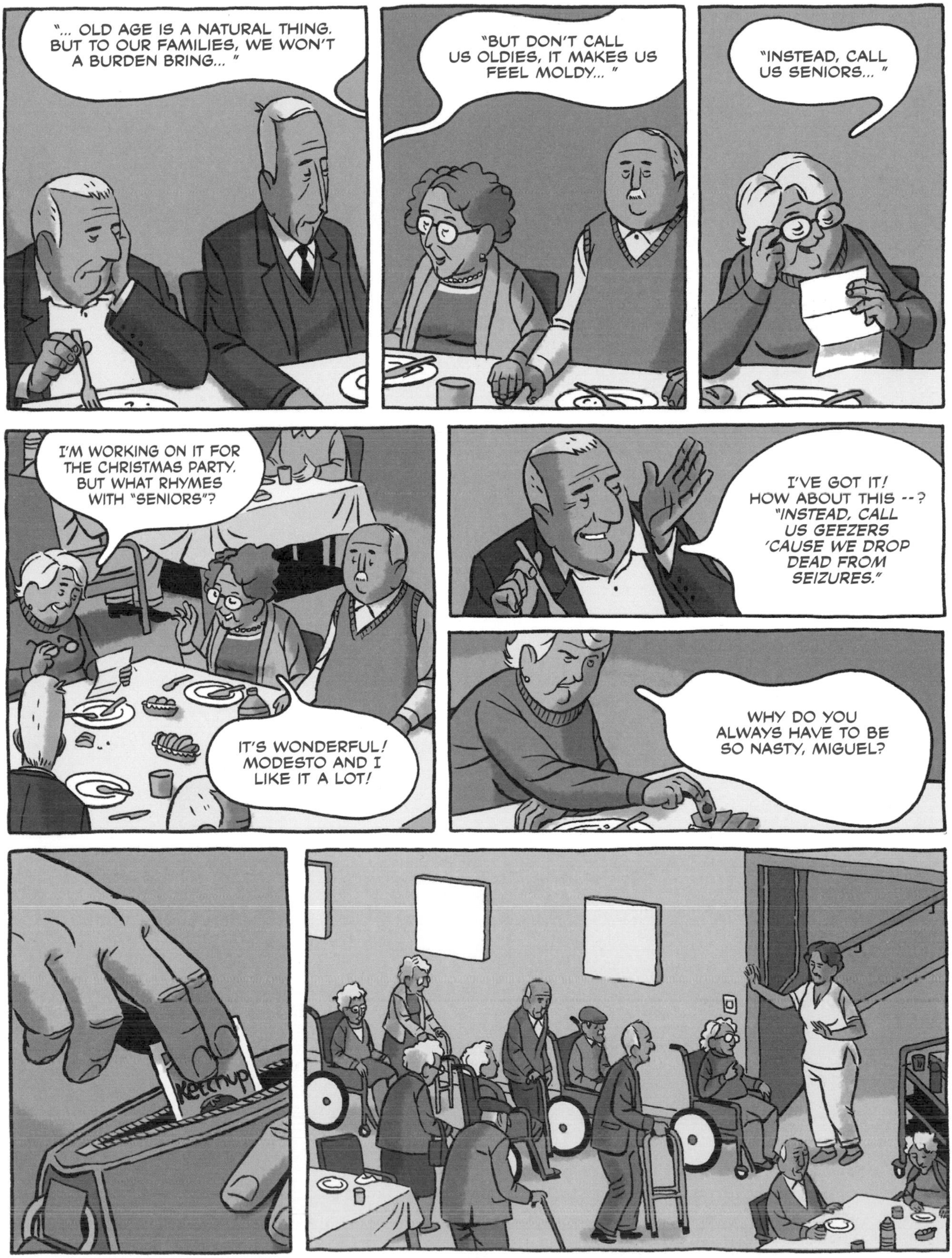
"... OLD AGE IS A NATURAL THING. BUT TO OUR FAMILIES, WE WON'T A BURDEN BRING... "
"BUT DON'T CALL US OLDIES, IT MAKES US FEEL MOLDY... "
"INSTEAD, CALL US SENIORS... "
I'M WORKING ON IT FOR THE CHRISTMAS PARTY. BUT WHAT RHYMES WITH "SENIORS"?
IT'S WONDERFUL! MODESTO AND I LIKE IT A LOT!
I'VE GOT IT! HOW ABOUT THIS --? "INSTEAD, CALL US GEEZERS 'CAUSE WE DROP DEAD FROM SEIZURES."
WHY DO YOU ALWAYS HAVE TO BE SO NASTY, MIGUEL?
Ketchup

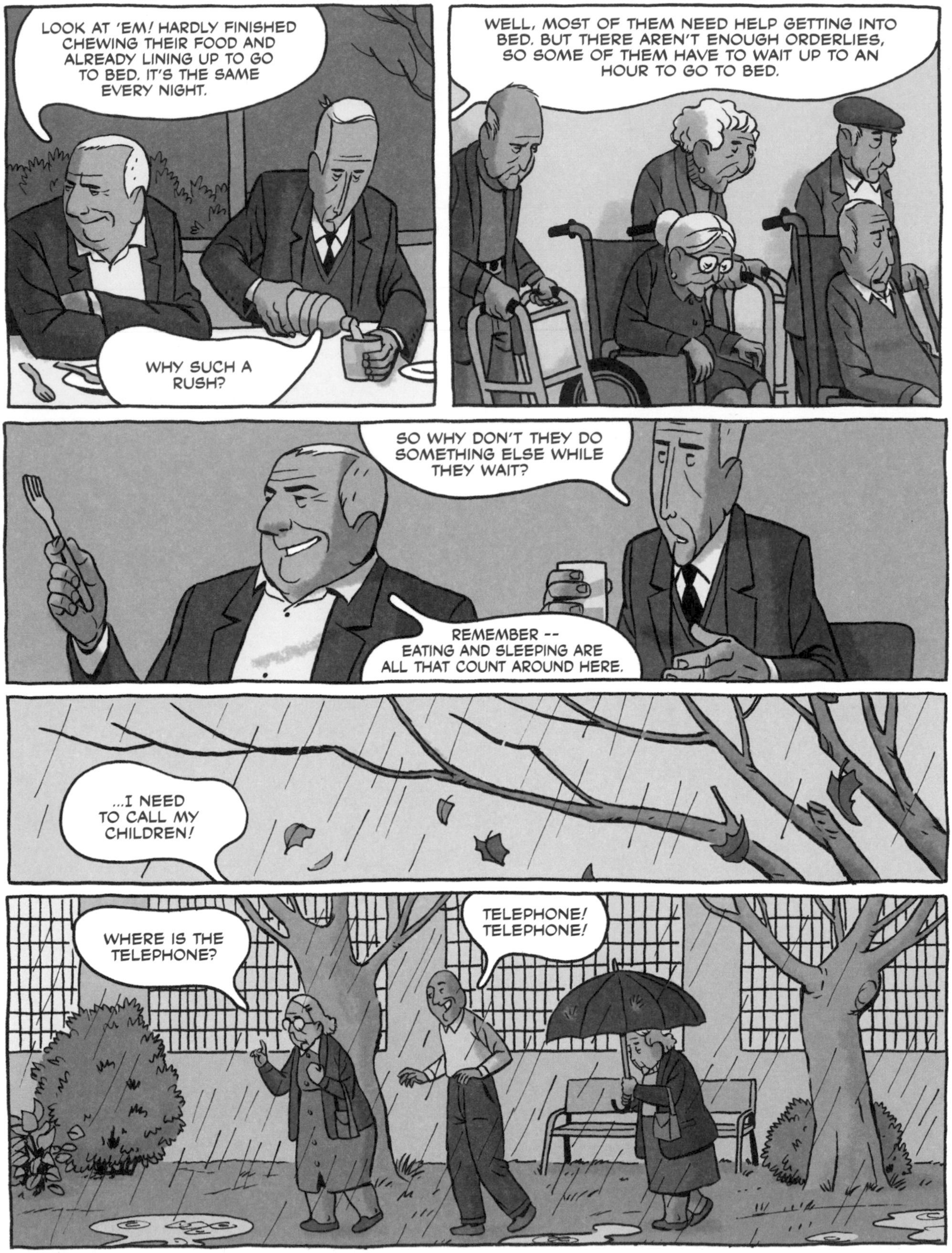
LOOK AT 'EM! HARDLY FINISHED CHEWING THEIR FOOD AND ALREADY LINING UP TO GO TO BED. IT'S THE SAME EVERY NIGHT.
WHY SUCH A RUSH?
WELL, MOST OF THEM NEED HELP GETTING INTO BED. BUT THERE AREN'T ENOUGH ORDERLIES, SO SOME OF THEM HAVE TO WAIT UP TO AN HOUR TO GO TO BED.
SO WHY DON'T THEY DO SOMETHING ELSE WHILE THEY WAIT?
REMEMBER -- EATING AND SLEEPING ARE ALL THAT COUNT AROUND HERE.
...I NEED TO CALL MY CHILDREN!
WHERE IS THE TELEPHONE?
TELEPHONE! TELEPHONE!

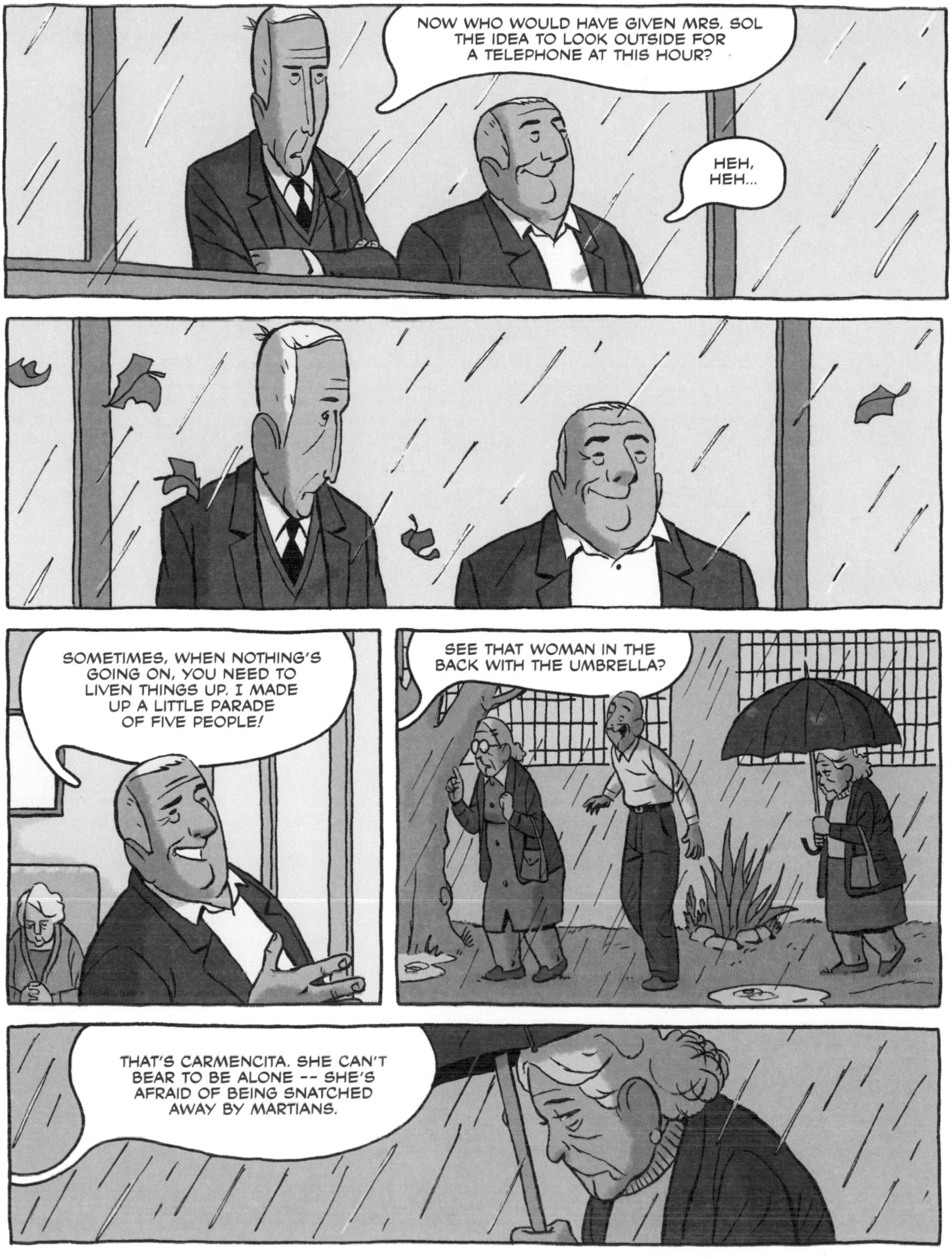
NOW WHO WOULD HAVE GIVEN MRS. SOL THE IDEA TO LOOK OUTSIDE FOR A TELEPHONE AT THIS HOUR?
HEH, HEH...
SOMETIMES, WHEN NOTHING'S GOING ON, YOU NEED TO LIVEN THINGS UP. I MADE UP A LITTLE PARADE OF FIVE PEOPLE!
SEE THAT WOMAN IN THE BACK WITH THE UMBRELLA?
THAT'S CARMENCITA. SHE CAN'T BEAR TO BE ALONE -- SHE'S AFRAID OF BEING SNATCHED AWAY BY MARTIANS.

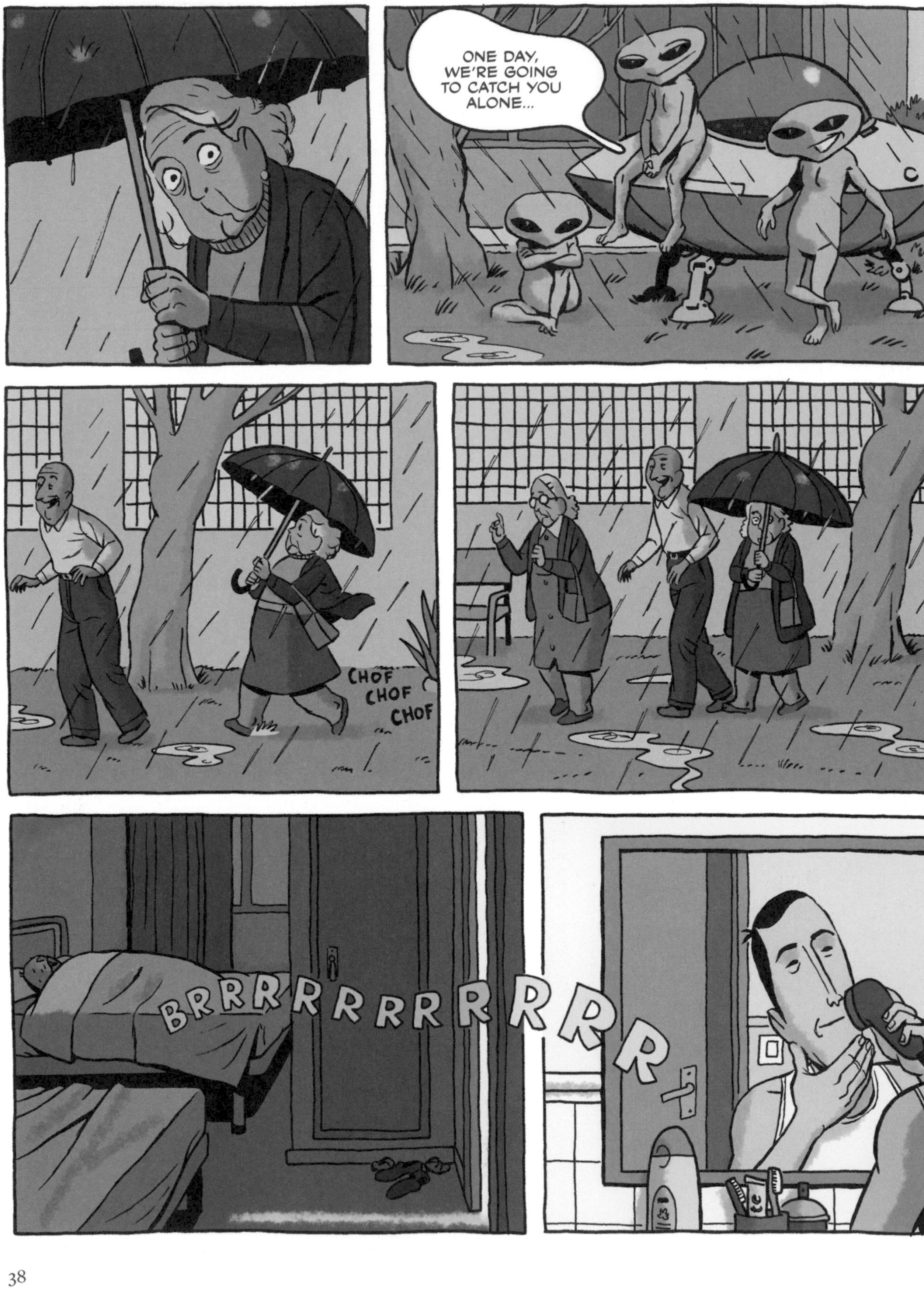
ONE DAY, WE'RE GOING TO CATCH YOU ALONE...
CHOF
CHOF
CHOF
BRRRRRRRRRRRR-

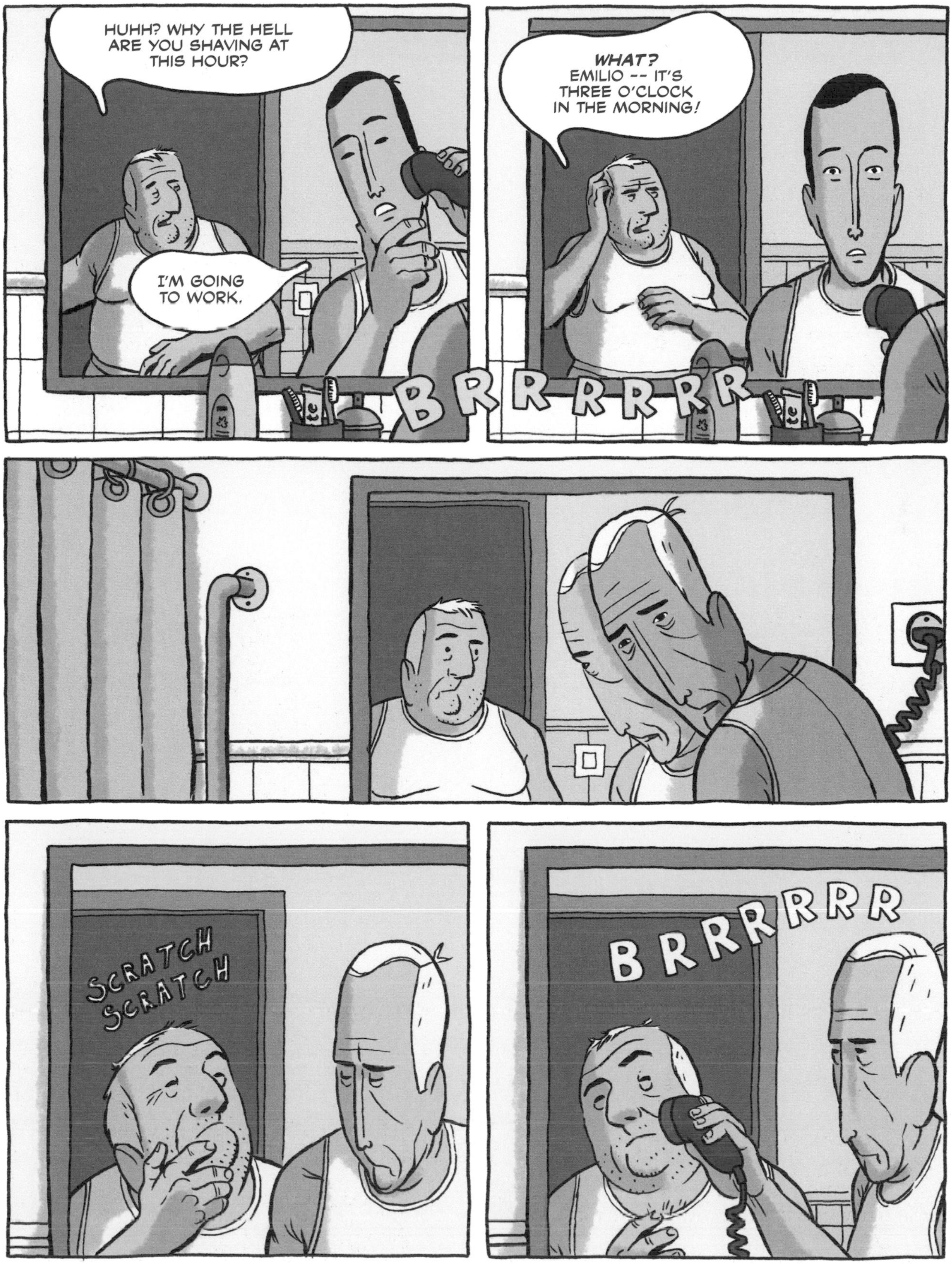
HUHH? WHY THE HELL ARE YOU SHAVING AT THIS HOUR?
I'M GOING TO WORK.
BRRRRRR
WHAT? EMILIO -- IT'S THREE O'CLOCK IN THE MORNING!
SCRATCH SCRATCH
BRRRRRRR

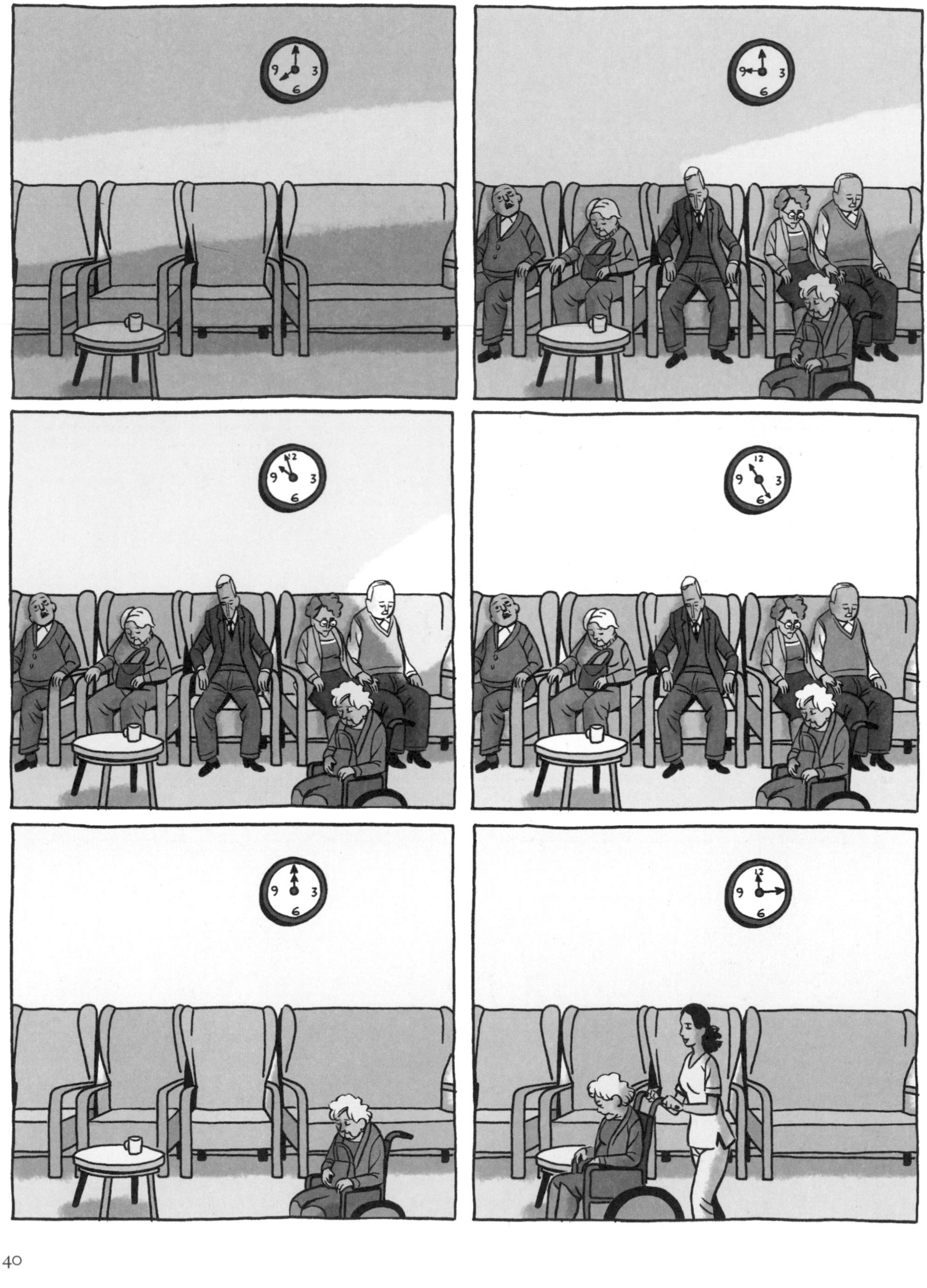

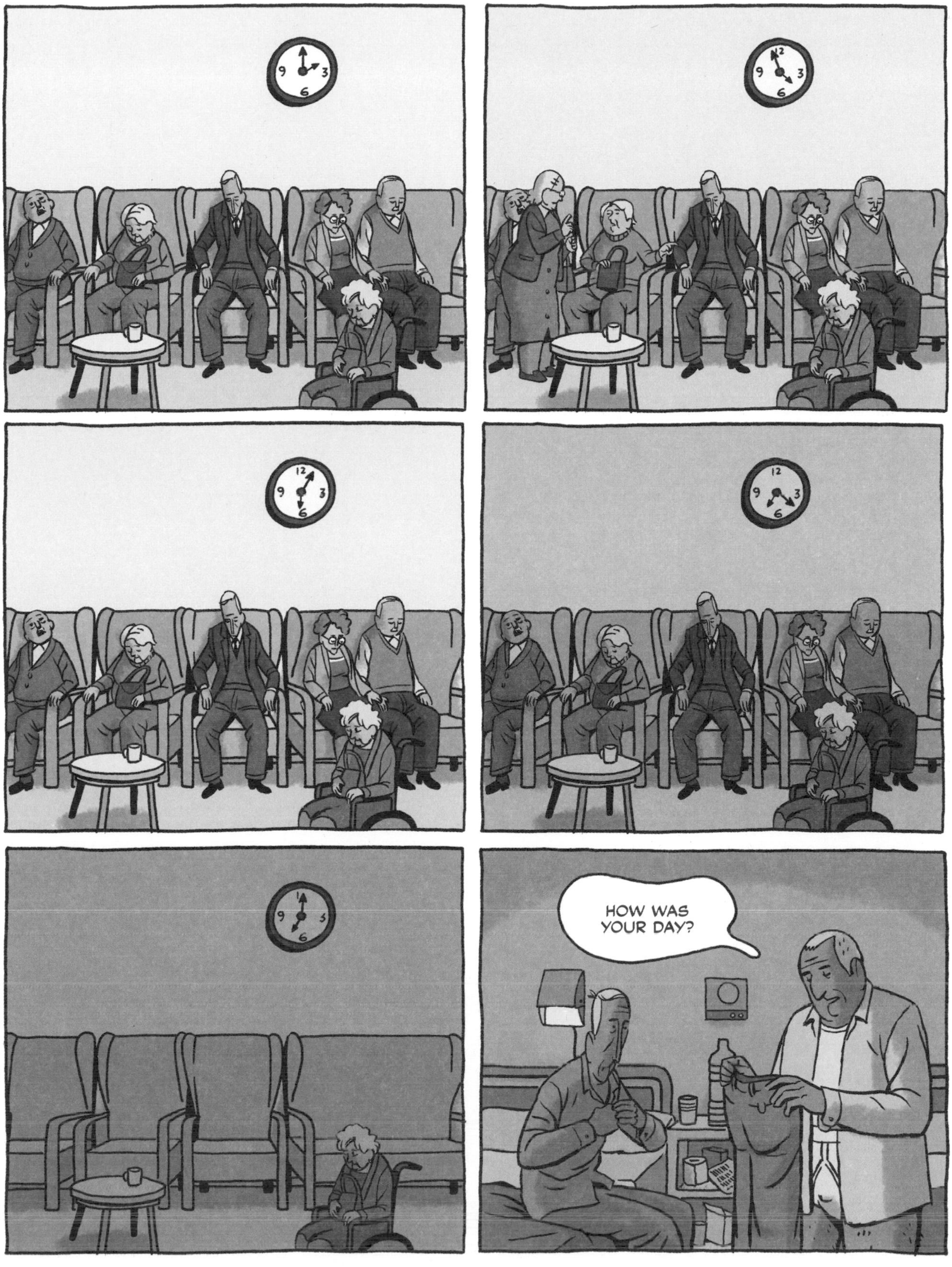
HOW WAS
YOUR DAY?

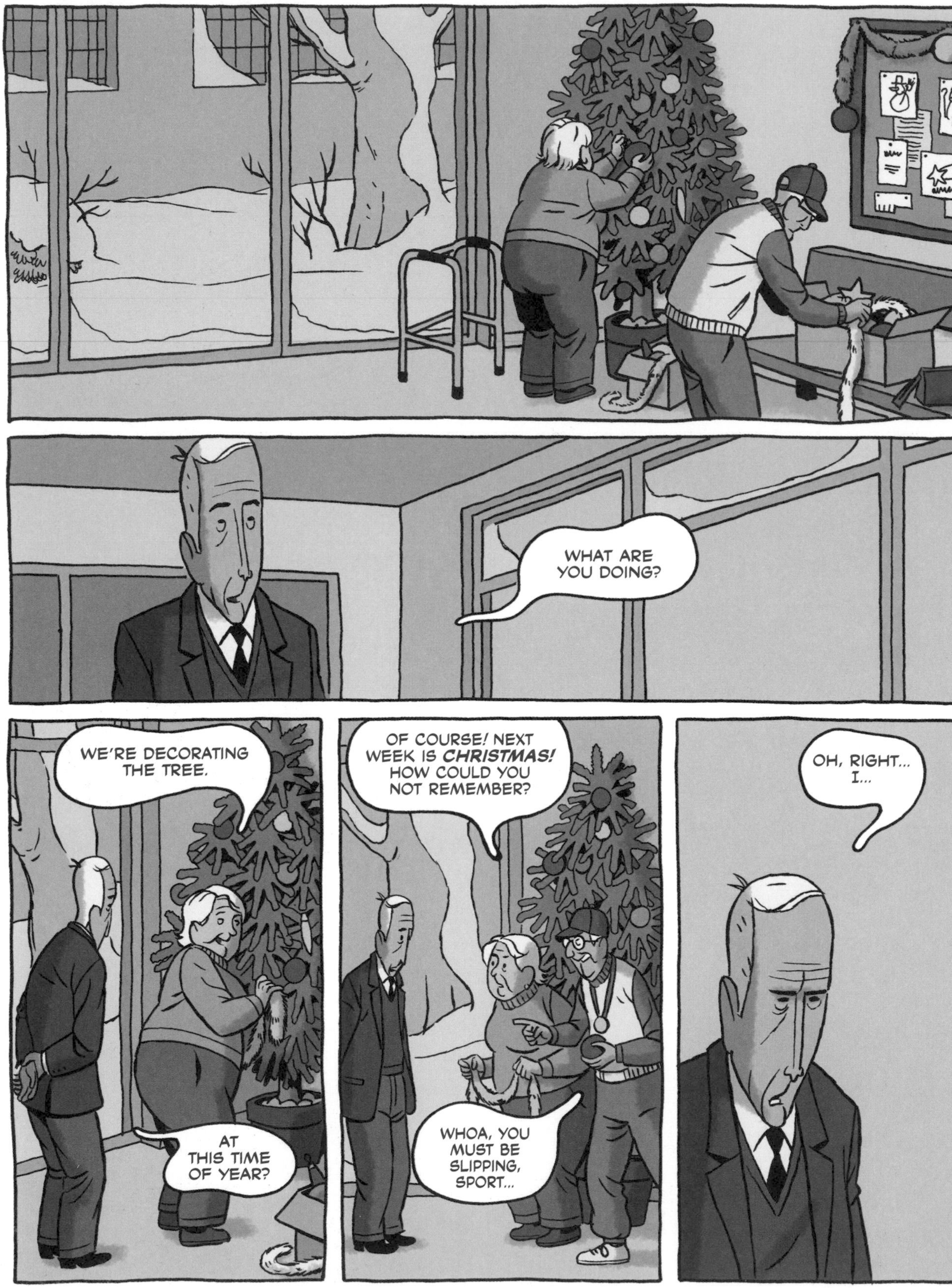
WHAT ARE YOU DOING?
WE'RE DECORATING THE TREE.
AT THIS TIME OF YEAR?
OF COURSE! NEXT WEEK IS CHRISTMAS! HOW COULD YOU NOT REMEMBER?
WHOA, YOU MUST BE SLIPPING, SPORT...
OH, RIGHT... I...

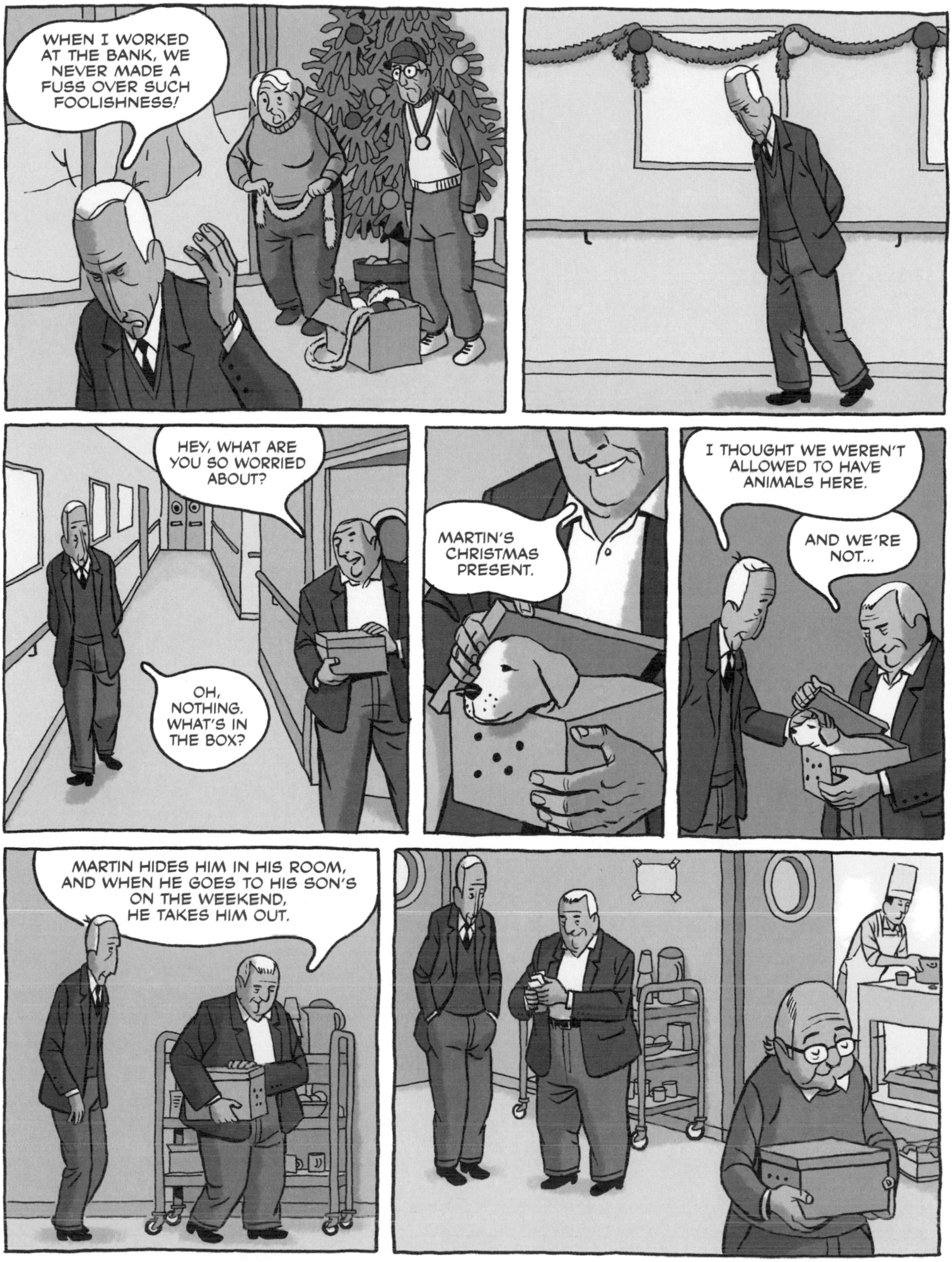

WHEN I WORKED AT THE BANK, WE NEVER MADE A FUSS OVER SUCH FOOLISHNESS!
HEY, WHAT ARE YOU SO WORRIED ABOUT?
OH, NOTHING. WHAT'S IN THE BOX?
MARTIN'S CHRISTMAS PRESENT.
I THOUGHT WE WEREN'T ALLOWED TO HAVE ANIMALS HERE.
AND WE'RE NOT...
MARTIN HIDES HIM IN HIS ROOM, AND WHEN HE GOES TO HIS SON'S ON THE WEEKEND, HE TAKES HIM OUT.

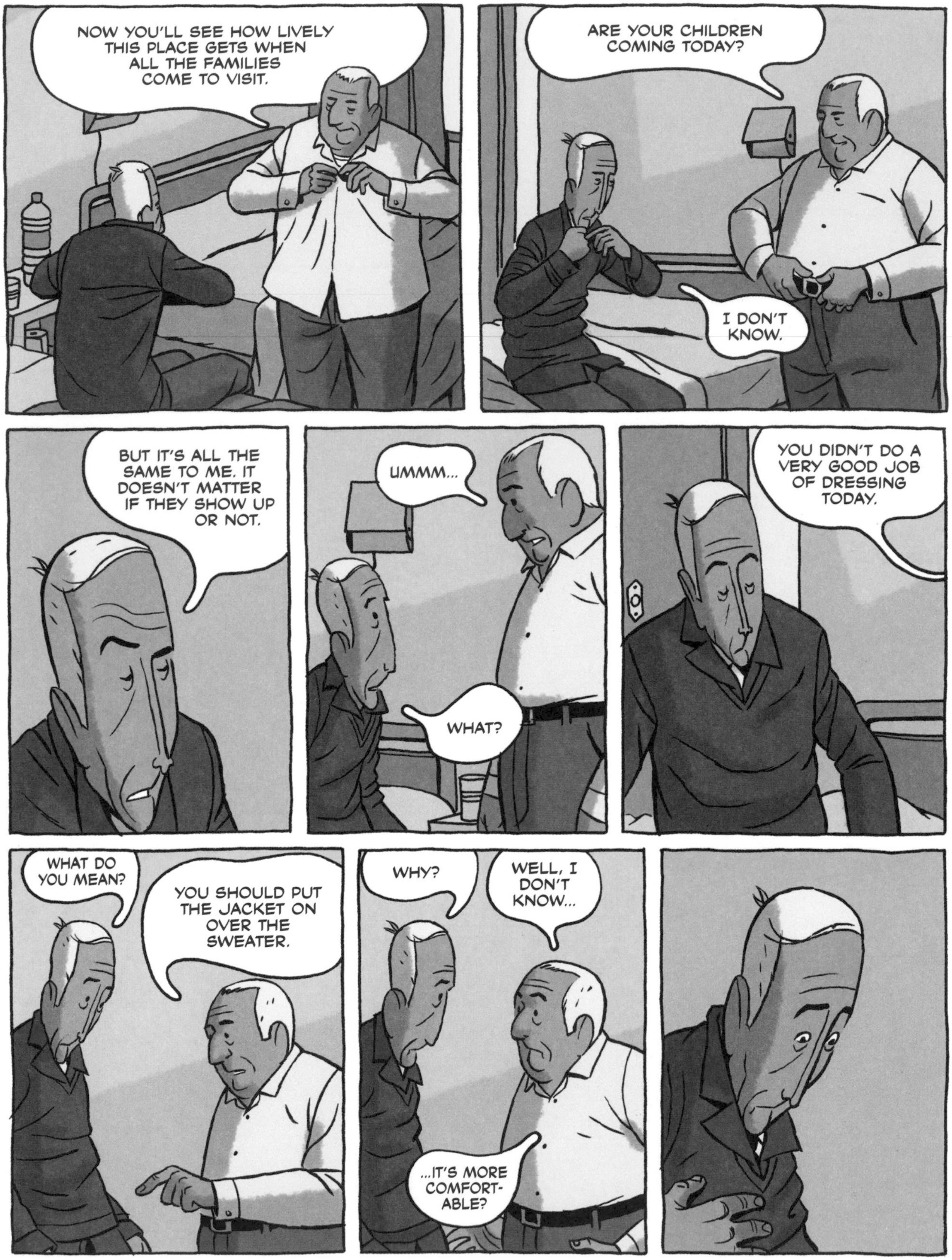
NOW YOU'LL SEE HOW LIVELY THIS PLACE GETS WHEN ALL THE FAMILIES COME TO VISIT.
ARE YOUR CHILDREN COMING TODAY?
I DON'T KNOW.
BUT IT'S ALL THE SAME TO ME. IT DOESN'T MATTER IF THEY SHOW UP OR NOT.
UMMM...
WHAT?
YOU DIDN'T DO A VERY GOOD JOB OF DRESSING TODAY.
WHAT DO YOU MEAN?
YOU SHOULD PUT THE JACKET ON OVER THE SWEATER.
WHY?
WELL, I DON'T KNOW...
...IT'S MORE COMFORT-ABLE?

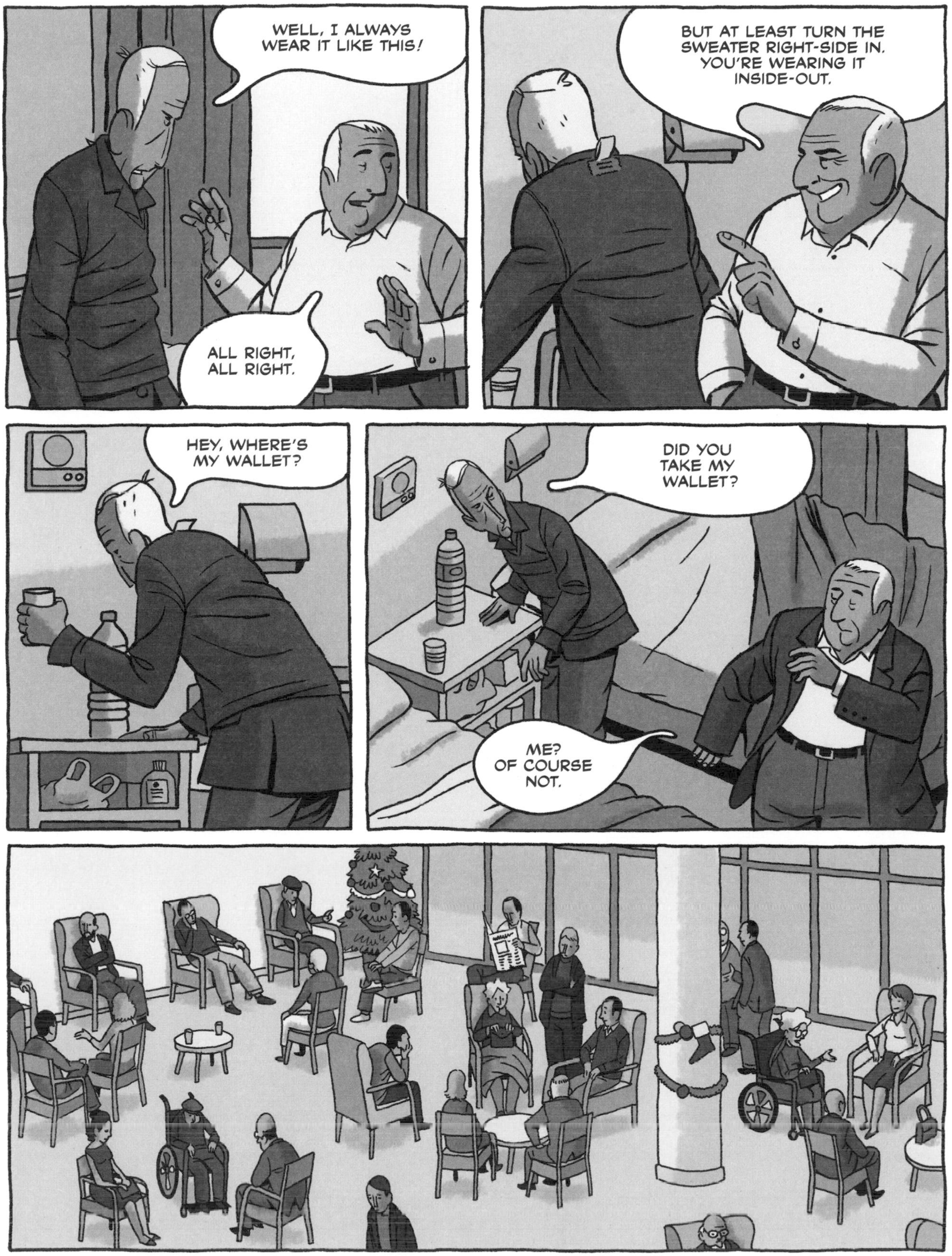
WELL, I ALWAYS WEAR IT LIKE THIS!
ALL RIGHT, ALL RIGHT.
BUT AT LEAST TURN THE SWEATER RIGHT-SIDE IN. YOU'RE WEARING IT INSIDE-OUT.
HEY, WHERE'S MY WALLET?
DID YOU TAKE MY WALLET?
ME? OF COURSE NOT.

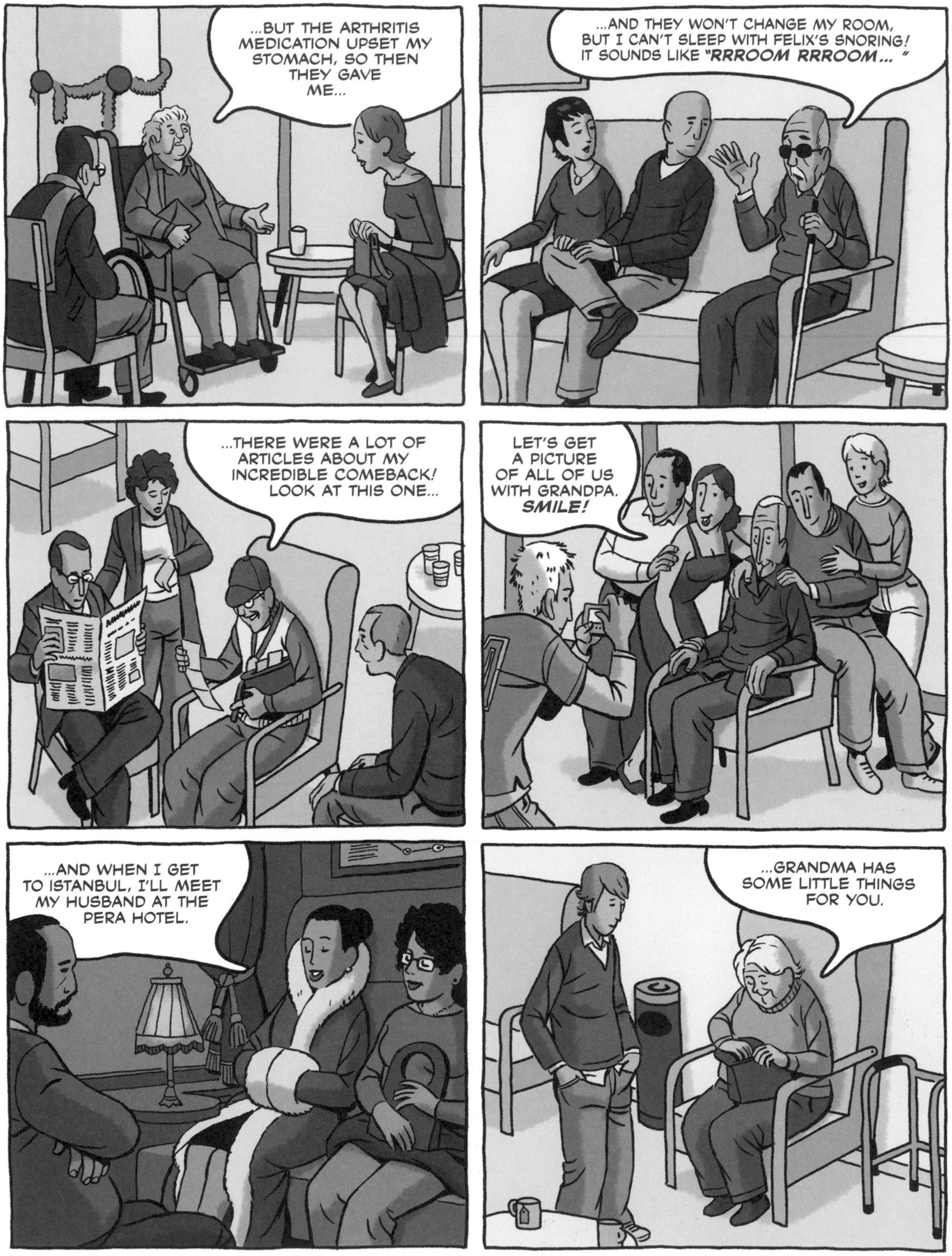
...BUT THE ARTHRITIS MEDICATION UPSET MY STOMACH, SO THEN THEY GAVE ME...
...AND THEY WON'T CHANGE MY ROOM, BUT I CAN'T SLEEP WITH FELIX'S SNORING! IT SOUNDS LIKE "RRROOM RRROOM... "
...THERE WERE A LOT OF ARTICLES ABOUT MY INCREDIBLE COMEBACK! LOOK AT THIS ONE...
LET'S GET A PICTURE OF ALL OF US WITH GRANDPA. SMILE!
...AND WHEN I GET TO ISTANBUL, I'LL MEET MY HUSBAND AT THE PERA HOTEL.
...GRANDMA HAS SOME LITTLE THINGS FOR YOU.

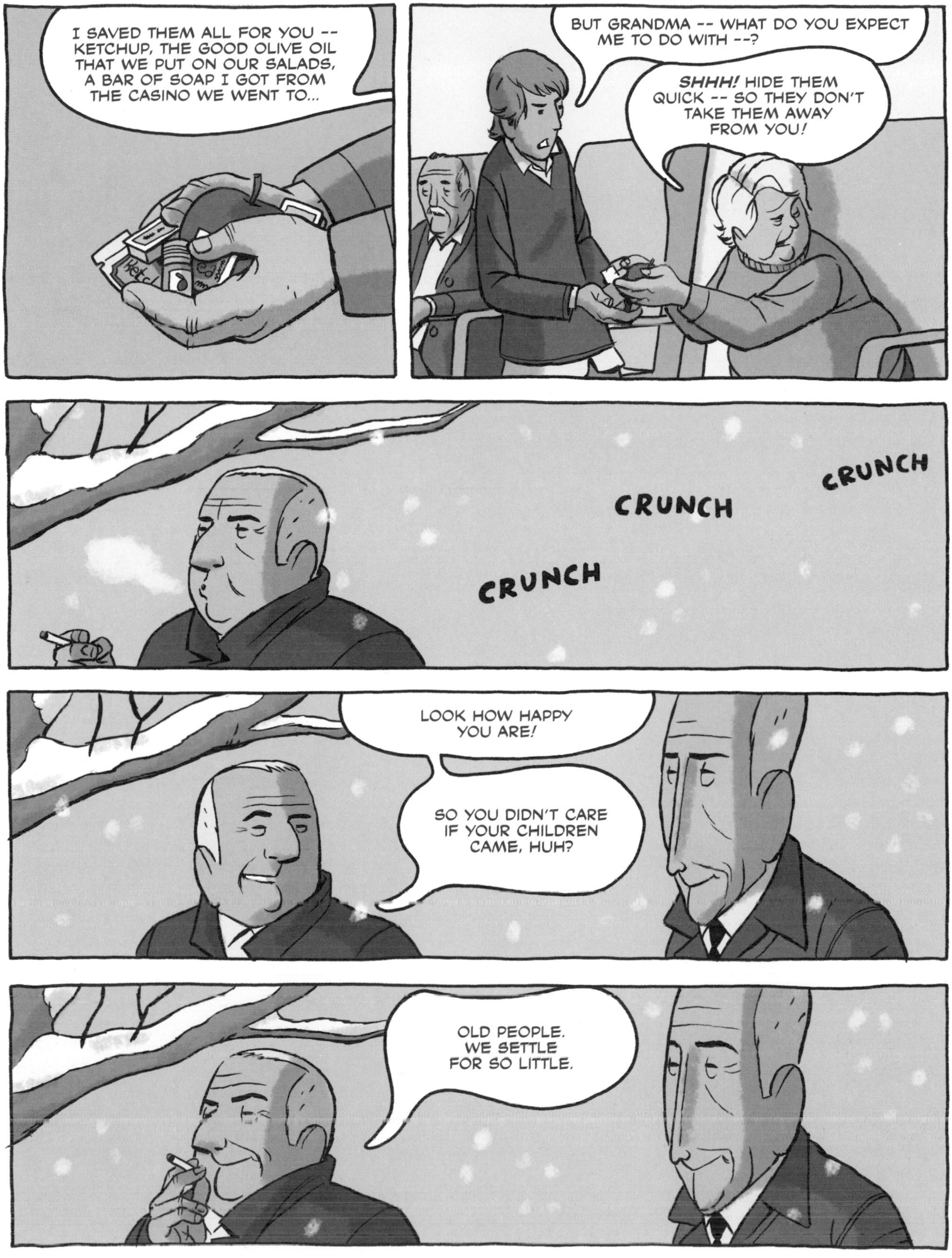
I SAVED THEM ALL FOR YOU -- KETCHUP, THE GOOD OLIVE OIL THAT WE PUT ON OUR SALADS, A BAR OF SOAP I GOT FROM THE CASINO WE WENT TO...
BUT GRANDMA -- WHAT DO YOU EXPECT ME TO DO WITH --?
SHHH! HIDE THEM QUICK -- SO THEY DON'T TAKE THEM AWAY FROM YOU!
CRUNCH
CRUNCH
CRUNCH
LOOK HOW HAPPY YOU ARE!
SO YOU DIDN'T CARE IF YOUR CHILDREN CAME, HUH?
OLD PEOPLE. WE SETTLE FOR SO LITTLE.

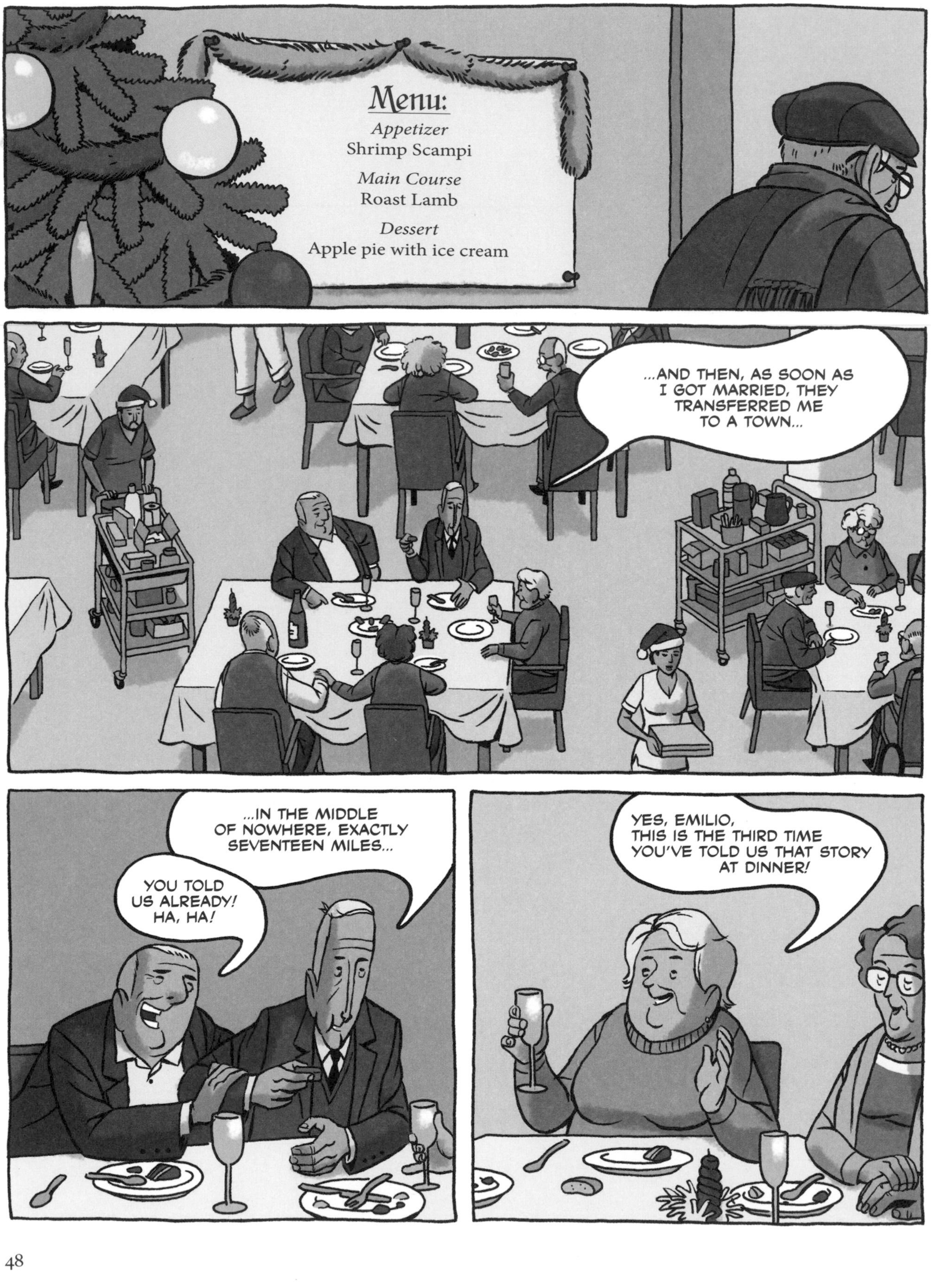
Menu:
Appetizer
Shrimp Scampi
Main Course
Roast Lamb
Dessert
Apple pie with ice cream
...AND THEN, AS SOON AS I GOT MARRIED, THEY TRANSFERRED ME TO A TOWN...
...IN THE MIDDLE OF NOWHERE, EXACTLY SEVENTEEN MILES...
YOU TOLD US ALREADY! HA, HA!
YES, EMILIO, THIS IS THE THIRD TIME YOU'VE TOLD US THAT STORY AT DINNER!

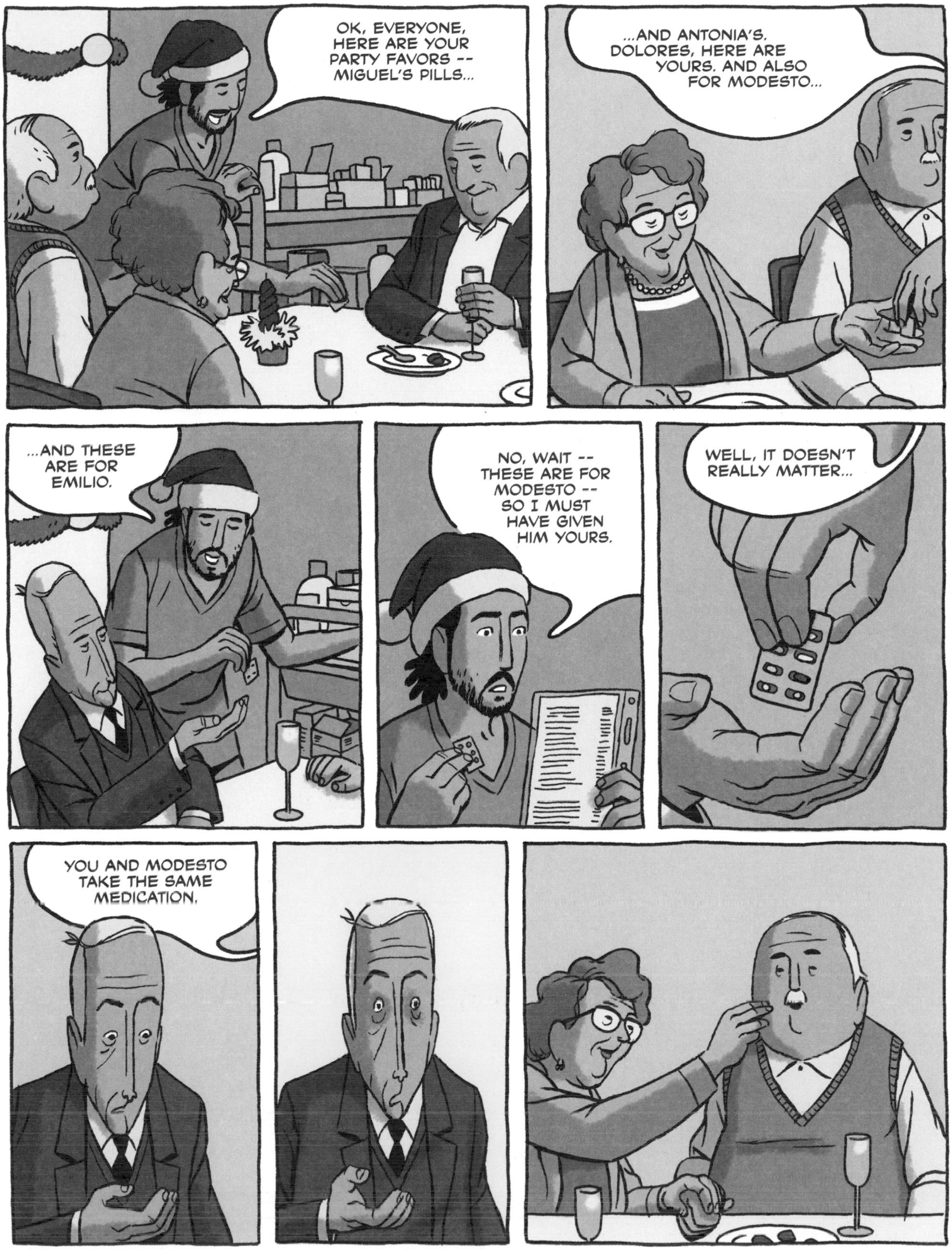
OK, EVERYONE, HERE ARE YOUR PARTY FAVORS -- MIGUEL'S PILLS...
...AND ANTONIA'S. DOLORES, HERE ARE YOURS. AND ALSO FOR MODESTO...
...AND THESE ARE FOR EMILIO.
NO, WAIT -- THESE ARE FOR MODESTO -- SO I MUST HAVE GIVEN HIM YOURS.
WELL, IT DOESN'T REALLY MATTER...
YOU AND MODESTO TAKE THE SAME MEDICATION.

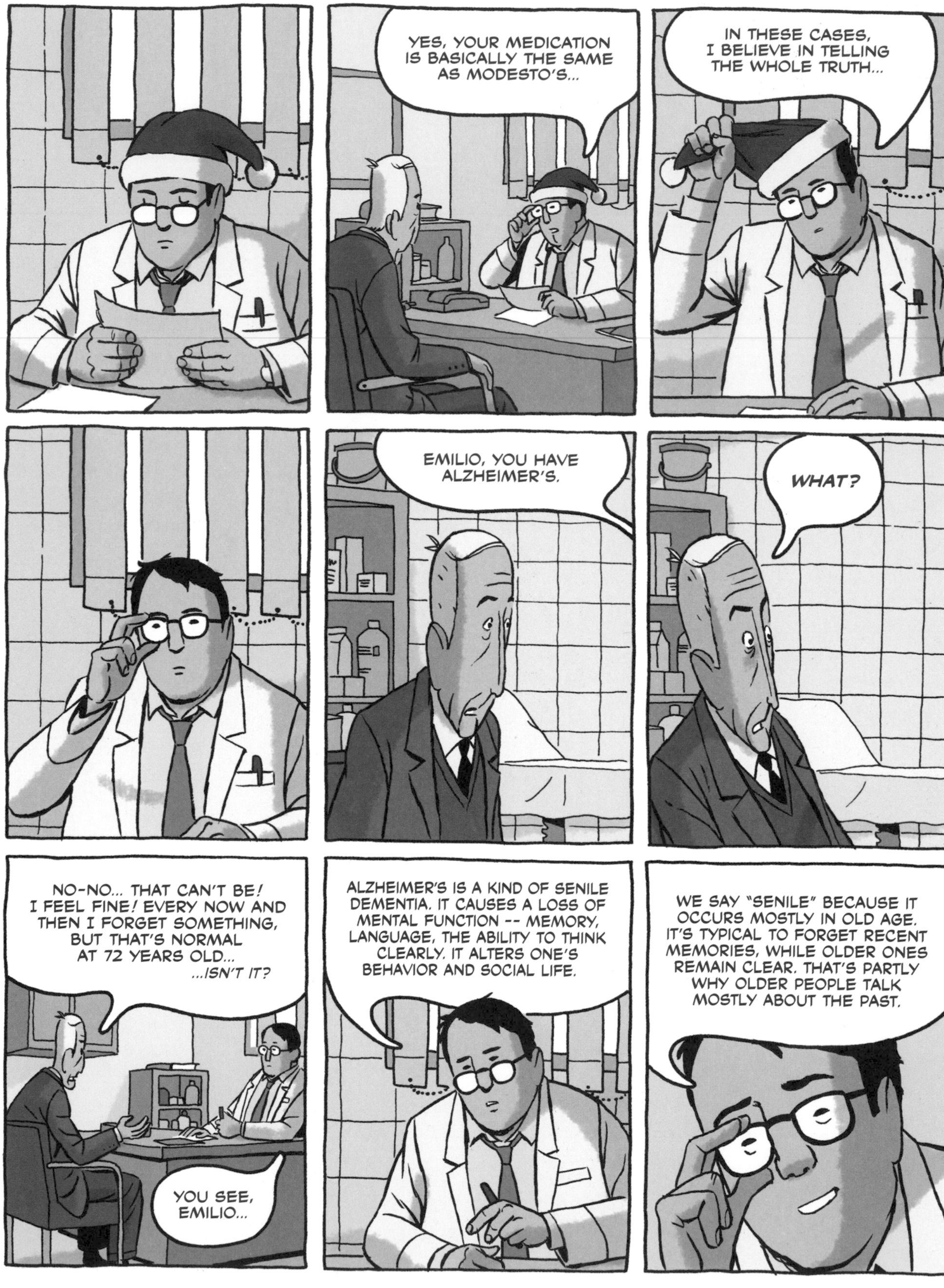
YES, YOUR MEDICATION IS BASICALLY THE SAME AS MODESTO'S...
IN THESE CASES, I BELIEVE IN TELLING THE WHOLE TRUTH...
EMILIO, YOU HAVE ALZHEIMER'S.
WHAT?
NO-NO... THAT CAN'T BE! I FEEL FINE! EVERY NOW AND THEN I FORGET SOMETHING, BUT THAT'S NORMAL AT 72 YEARS OLD...
...ISN'T IT?
YOU SEE, EMILIO...
ALZHEIMER'S IS A KIND OF SENILE DEMENTIA. IT CAUSES A LOSS OF MENTAL FUNCTION -- MEMORY, LANGUAGE, THE ABILITY TO THINK CLEARLY. IT ALTERS ONE'S BEHAVIOR AND SOCIAL LIFE.
WE SAY "SENILE" BECAUSE IT OCCURS MOSTLY IN OLD AGE. IT'S TYPICAL TO FORGET RECENT MEMORIES, WHILE OLDER ONES REMAIN CLEAR. THAT'S PARTLY WHY OLDER PEOPLE TALK MOSTLY ABOUT THE PAST.

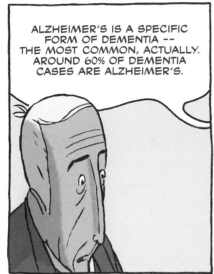

ALZHEIMER'S IS A SPECIFIC FORM OF DEMENTIA -- THE MOST COMMON, ACTUALLY. AROUND 60% OF DEMENTIA CASES ARE ALZHEIMER'S.

BUT IT IS PROGRESSIVE, AND IT WILL ULTIMATELY DESTROY OLD MEMORIES, AWARENESS OF PLACE, LANGUAGE, AND THE ABILITY TO TAKE CARE OF ONE'S SELF AND ACT INDEPENDENTLY.

BUT THAT'S NOT ME AT ALL. I'M JUST A LITTLE FORGETFUL. I'M NOT LIKE MODESTO.

FOR NOW...

I'M SORRY TO HAVE TO TELL YOU THIS, EMILIO, BUT YOU'RE IN THE EARLY STAGES. AND WE HAVE NO WAY TO REVERSE IT. IT'S VERY DIFFICULT FOR THE PATIENT AND FOR THE FAMILY.

HOW... HOW LONG...?

WE CAN TREAT YOU TO IMPROVE YOUR QUALITY OF LIFE OVER THE NEXT FEW YEARS.

BUT... I'LL STILL END UP LIKE MODESTO?

EVERY PERSON IS DIFFERENT.

FIVE YEARS? EIGHT?

MAYBE MORE, MAYBE LESS. LIKE I SAID, EMILIO, EVERYONE IS DIFFERENT.

AND... WHAT... WHAT CAN I DO?

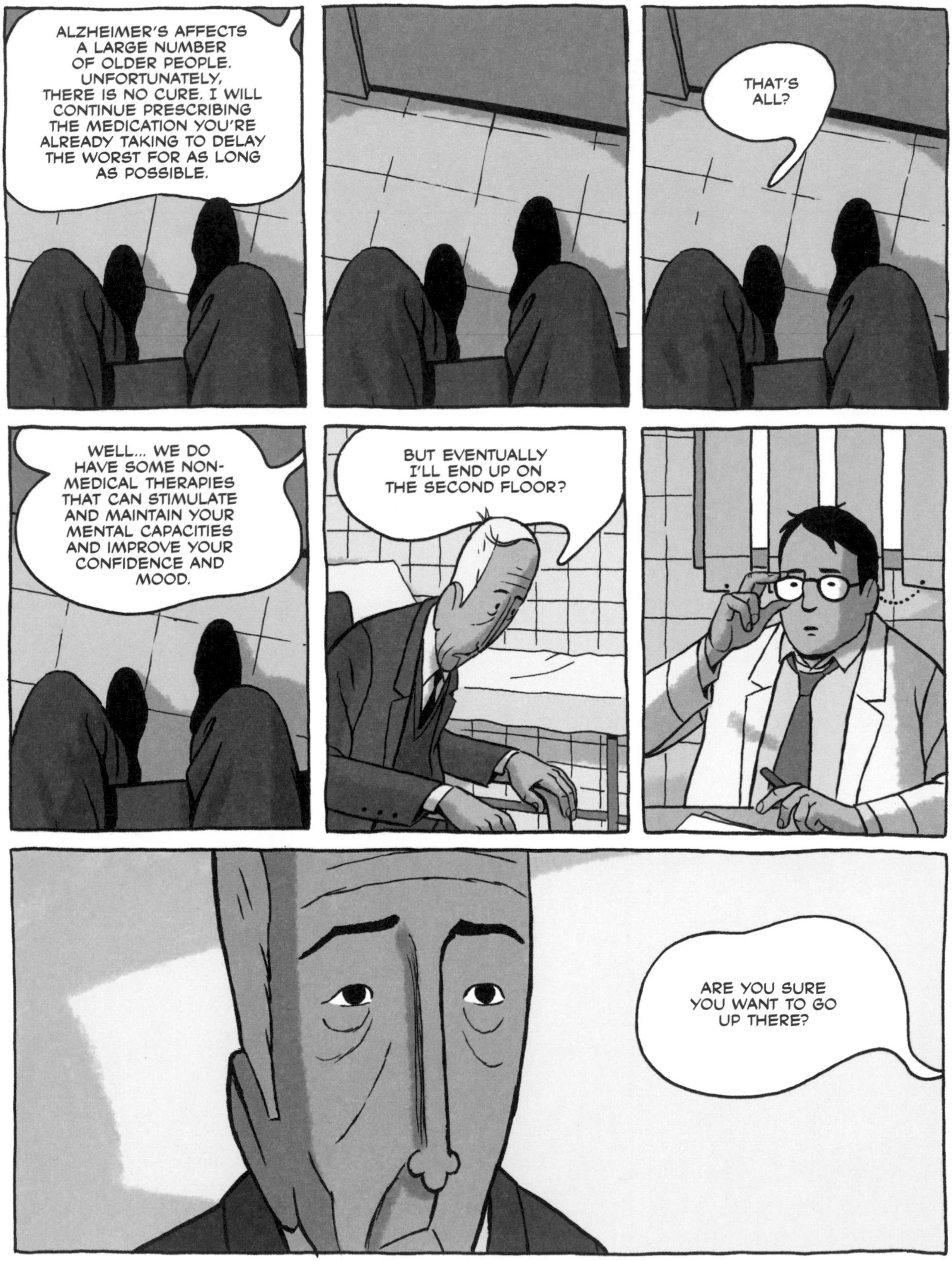
ALZHEIMER'S AFFECTS A LARGE NUMBER OF OLDER PEOPLE. UNFORTUNATELY, THERE IS NO CURE. I WILL CONTINUE PRESCRIBING THE MEDICATION YOU'RE ALREADY TAKING TO DELAY THE WORST FOR AS LONG AS POSSIBLE.
THAT'S ALL?
WELL... WE DO HAVE SOME NON-MEDICAL THERAPIES THAT CAN STIMULATE AND MAINTAIN YOUR MENTAL CAPACITIES AND IMPROVE YOUR CONFIDENCE AND MOOD.
BUT EVENTUALLY I'LL END UP ON THE SECOND FLOOR?
ARE YOU SURE YOU WANT TO GO UP THERE?

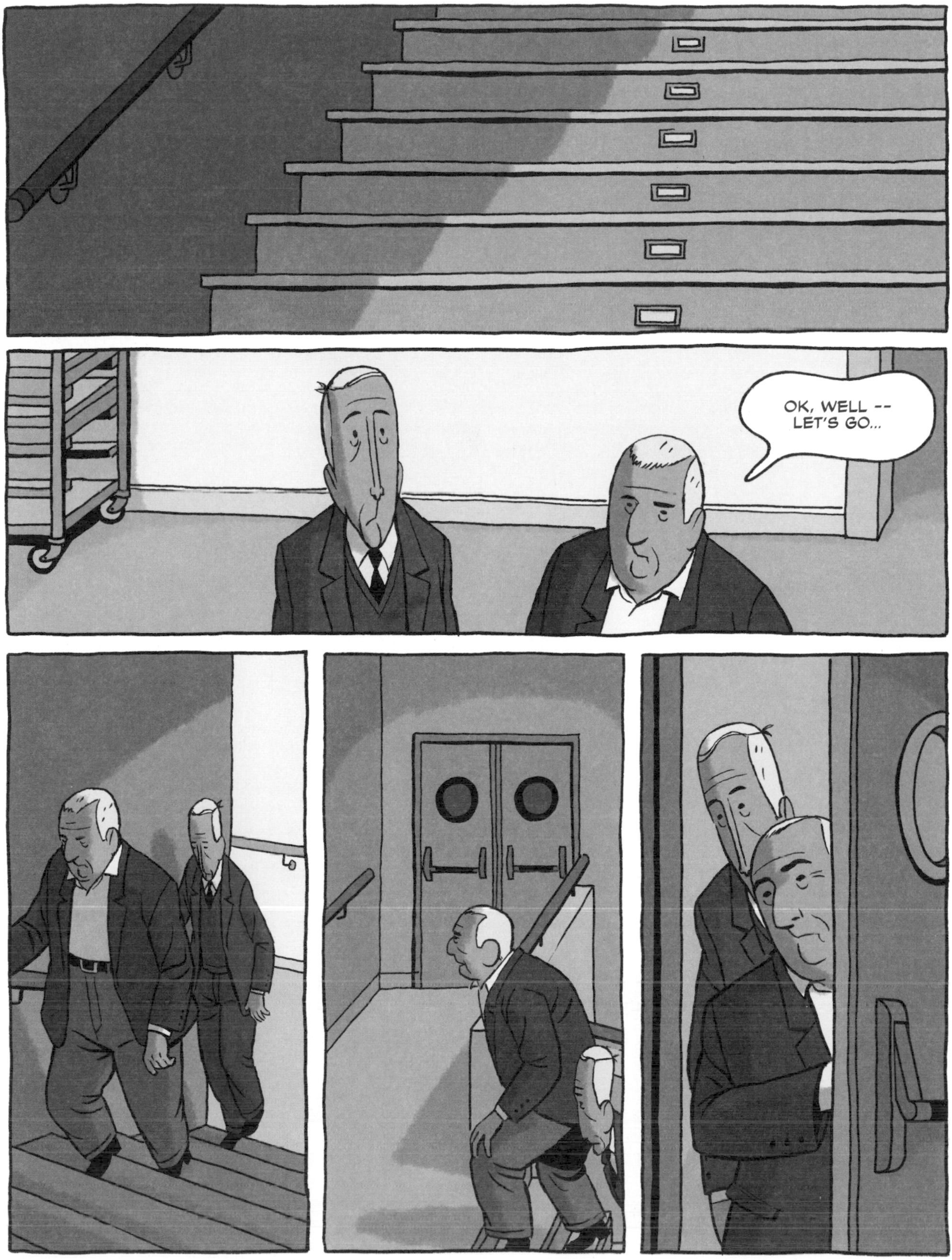
OK, WELL -- LET'S GO...

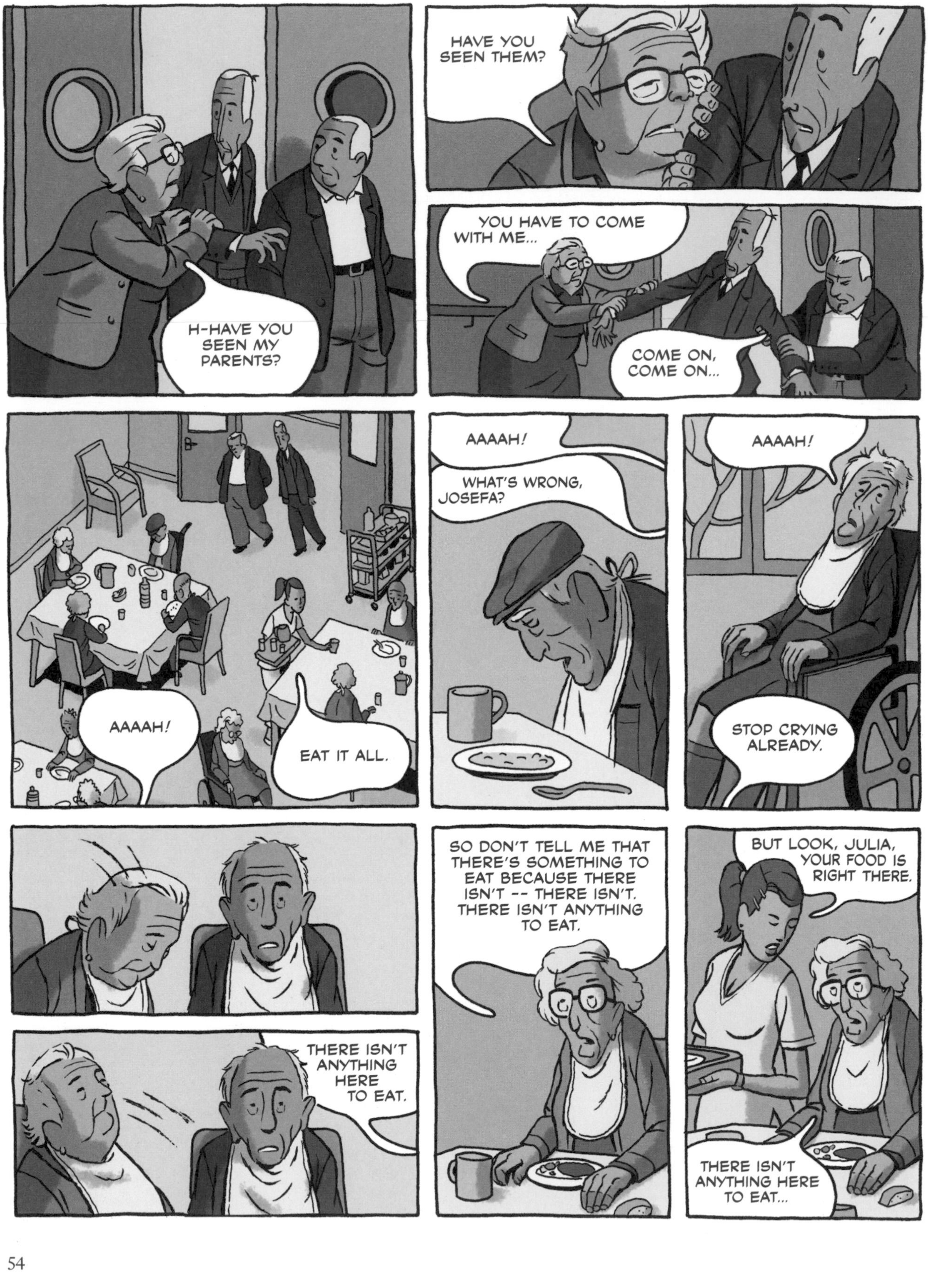
H-HAVE YOU SEEN MY PARENTS?
HAVE YOU SEEN THEM?
YOU HAVE TO COME WITH ME...
COME ON, COME ON...
AAAAH!
EAT IT ALL.
AAAAH!
WHAT'S WRONG, JOSEFA?
AAAAH!
STOP CRYING ALREADY.
THERE ISN'T ANYTHING HERE TO EAT.
SO DON'T TELL ME THAT THERE'S SOMETHING TO EAT BECAUSE THERE ISN'T -- THERE ISN'T. THERE ISN'T ANYTHING TO EAT.
BUT LOOK, JULIA, YOUR FOOD IS RIGHT THERE.
THERE ISN'T ANYTHING HERE TO EAT...

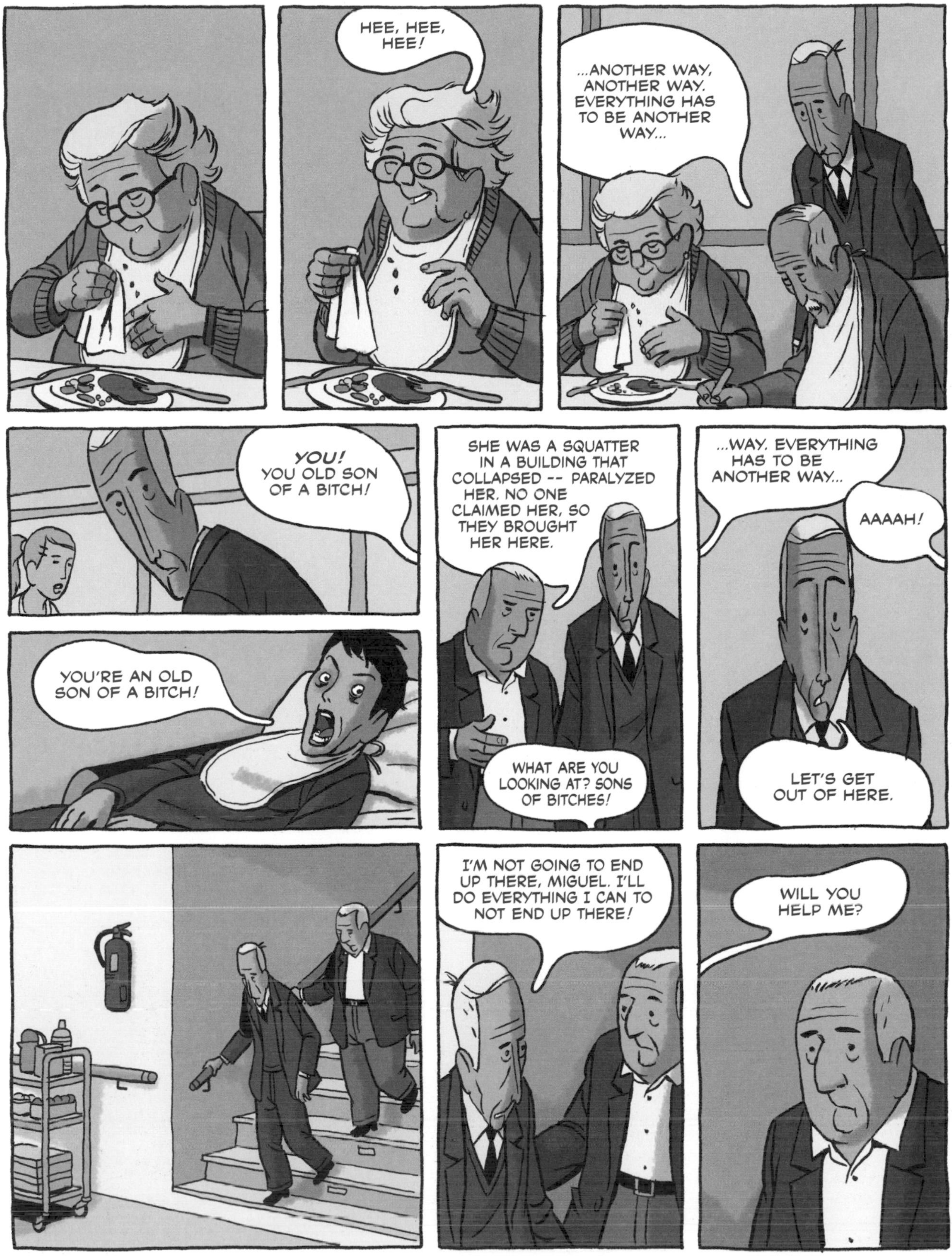
HEE, HEE, HEE!
...ANOTHER WAY, ANOTHER WAY. EVERYTHING HAS TO BE ANOTHER WAY...
YOU! YOU OLD SON OF A BITCH!
YOU'RE AN OLD SON OF A BITCH!
SHE WAS A SQUATTER IN A BUILDING THAT COLLAPSED -- PARALYZED HER. NO ONE CLAIMED HER, SO THEY BROUGHT HER HERE.
WHAT ARE YOU LOOKING AT? SONS OF BITCHES!
...WAY. EVERYTHING HAS TO BE ANOTHER WAY...
AAAAH!
LET'S GET OUT OF HERE.
I'M NOT GOING TO END UP THERE, MIGUEL. I'LL DO EVERYTHING I CAN TO NOT END UP THERE!
WILL YOU HELP ME?

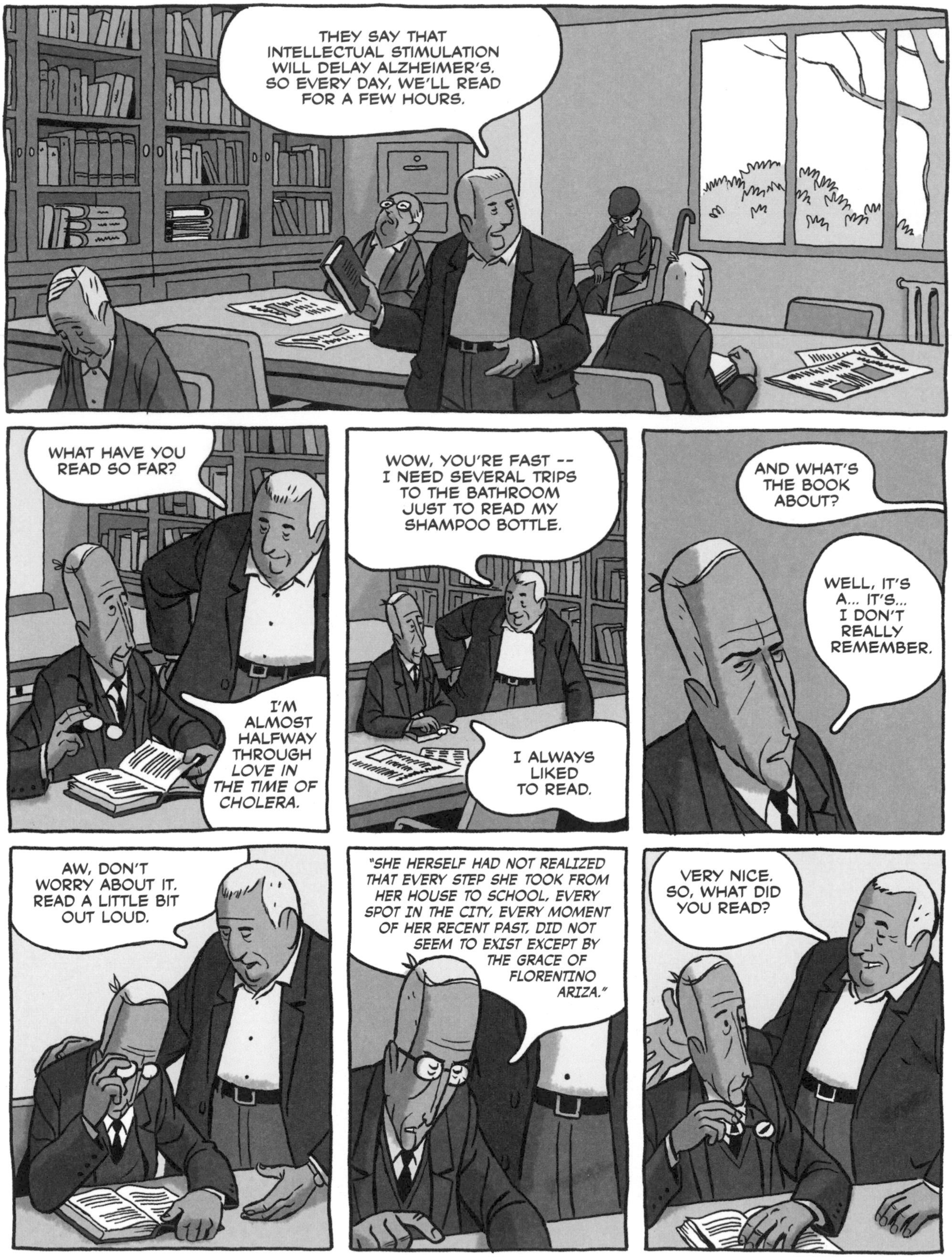
THEY SAY THAT INTELLECTUAL STIMULATION WILL DELAY ALZHEIMER'S. SO EVERY DAY, WE'LL READ FOR A FEW HOURS.
WHAT HAVE YOU READ SO FAR?
I'M ALMOST HALFWAY THROUGH *LOVE IN THE TIME OF CHOLERA.*
WOW, YOU'RE FAST -- I NEED SEVERAL TRIPS TO THE BATHROOM JUST TO READ MY SHAMPOO BOTTLE.
I ALWAYS LIKED TO READ.
AND WHAT'S THE BOOK ABOUT?
WELL, IT'S A... IT'S... I DON'T REALLY REMEMBER.
AW, DON'T WORRY ABOUT IT. READ A LITTLE BIT OUT LOUD.
"SHE HERSELF HAD NOT REALIZED THAT EVERY STEP SHE TOOK FROM HER HOUSE TO SCHOOL, EVERY SPOT IN THE CITY, EVERY MOMENT OF HER RECENT PAST, DID NOT SEEM TO EXIST EXCEPT BY THE GRACE OF FLORENTINO ARIZA."
VERY NICE. SO, WHAT DID YOU READ?

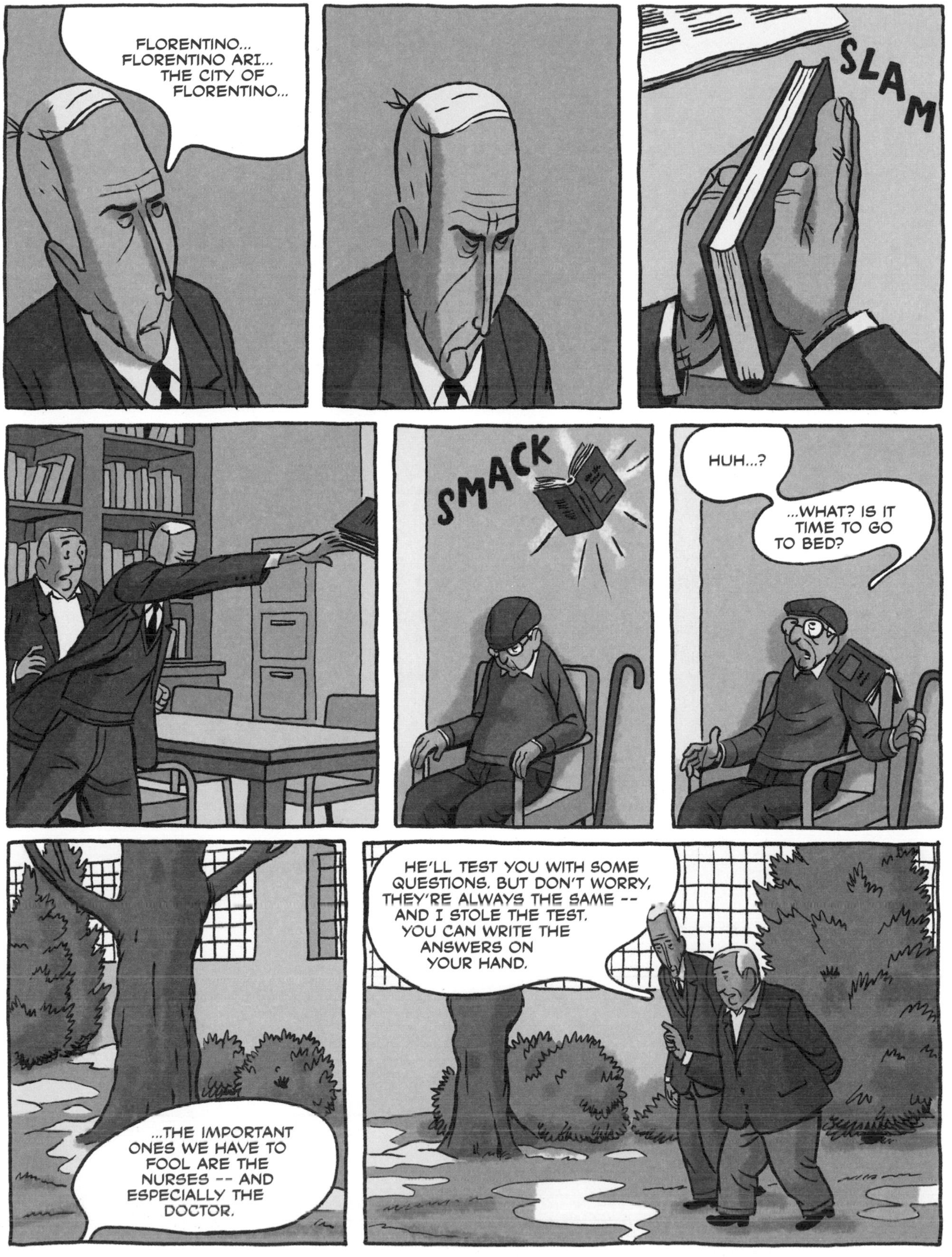

FLORENTINO... FLORENTINO ARI... THE CITY OF FLORENTINO...
SLAM
SMACK
HUH...?
...WHAT? IS IT TIME TO GO TO BED?
...THE IMPORTANT ONES WE HAVE TO FOOL ARE THE NURSES -- AND ESPECIALLY THE DOCTOR.
HE'LL TEST YOU WITH SOME QUESTIONS, BUT DON'T WORRY, THEY'RE ALWAYS THE SAME -- AND I STOLE THE TEST. YOU CAN WRITE THE ANSWERS ON YOUR HAND.

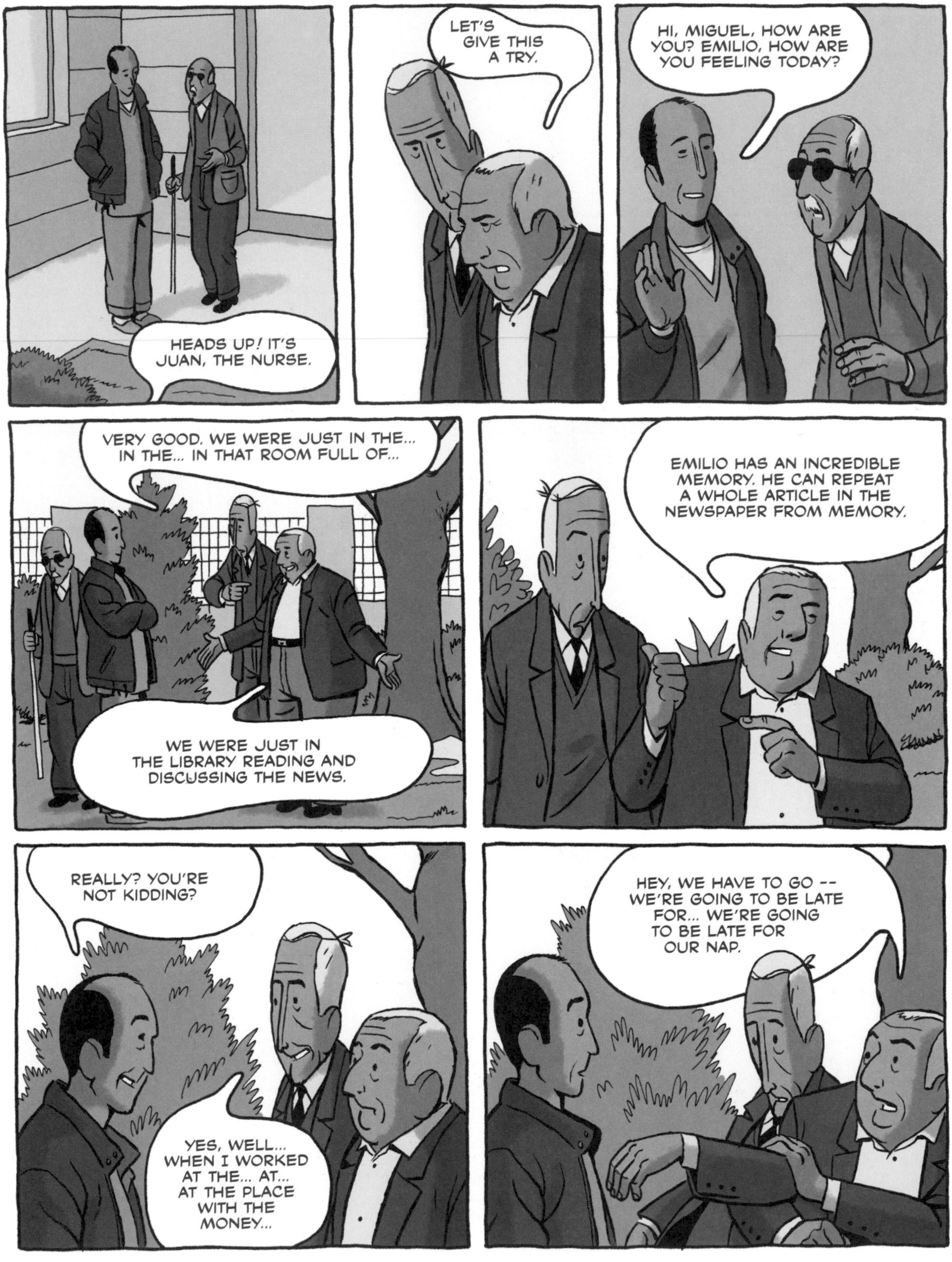
HEADS UP! IT'S JUAN, THE NURSE.
LET'S GIVE THIS A TRY.
HI, MIGUEL, HOW ARE YOU? EMILIO, HOW ARE YOU FEELING TODAY?
VERY GOOD. WE WERE JUST IN THE... IN THE... IN THAT ROOM FULL OF...
WE WERE JUST IN THE LIBRARY READING AND DISCUSSING THE NEWS.
EMILIO HAS AN INCREDIBLE MEMORY. HE CAN REPEAT A WHOLE ARTICLE IN THE NEWSPAPER FROM MEMORY.
REALLY? YOU'RE NOT KIDDING?
YES, WELL... WHEN I WORKED AT THE... AT... AT THE PLACE WITH THE MONEY...
HEY, WE HAVE TO GO -- WE'RE GOING TO BE LATE FOR... WE'RE GOING TO BE LATE FOR OUR NAP.

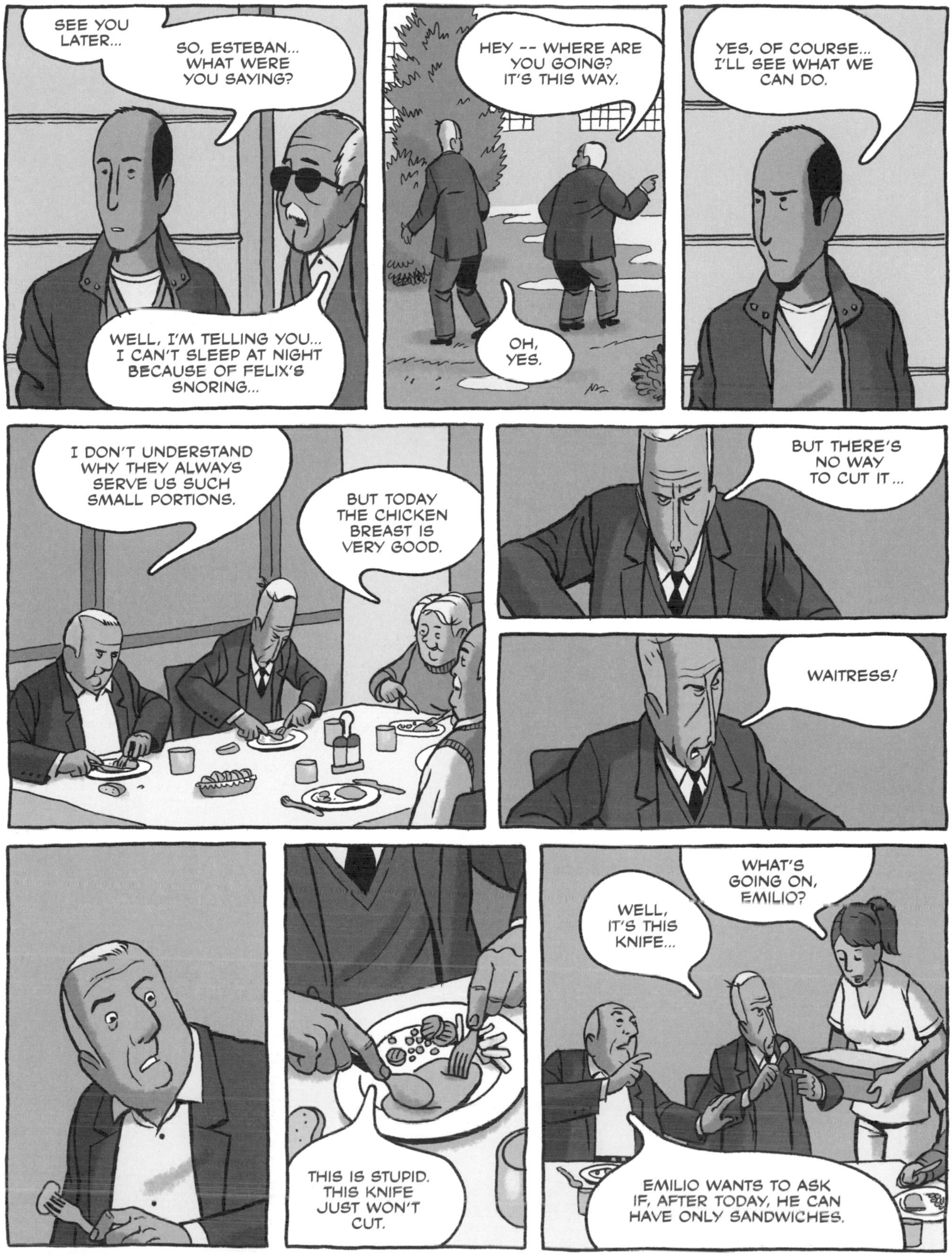
SEE YOU LATER...
SO, ESTEBAN... WHAT WERE YOU SAYING?
WELL, I'M TELLING YOU... I CAN'T SLEEP AT NIGHT BECAUSE OF FELIX'S SNORING...
HEY -- WHERE ARE YOU GOING? IT'S THIS WAY.
OH, YES.
YES, OF COURSE... I'LL SEE WHAT WE CAN DO.
I DON'T UNDERSTAND WHY THEY ALWAYS SERVE US SUCH SMALL PORTIONS.
BUT TODAY THE CHICKEN BREAST IS VERY GOOD.
BUT THERE'S NO WAY TO CUT IT...
WAITRESS!
THIS IS STUPID. THIS KNIFE JUST WON'T CUT.
WHAT'S GOING ON, EMILIO?
WELL, IT'S THIS KNIFE...
EMILIO WANTS TO ASK IF, AFTER TODAY, HE CAN HAVE ONLY SANDWICHES.

I'LL ASK IN THE KITCHEN. I DON'T THINK IT SHOULD BE A PROBLEM.

THANK YOU.

I... I... I DON'T KNOW WHY THEY MAKE SO MANY THINGS THAT LOOK ALIKE.

ARE THEY TRYING TO CONFUSE US?

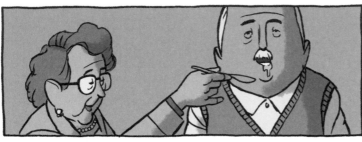

DOLORES, WHAT DO YOU SAY TO MODESTO TO MAKE HIM SMILE?

...

NOTHING REALLY. I SAY "CHEATER."

"CHEATER"?

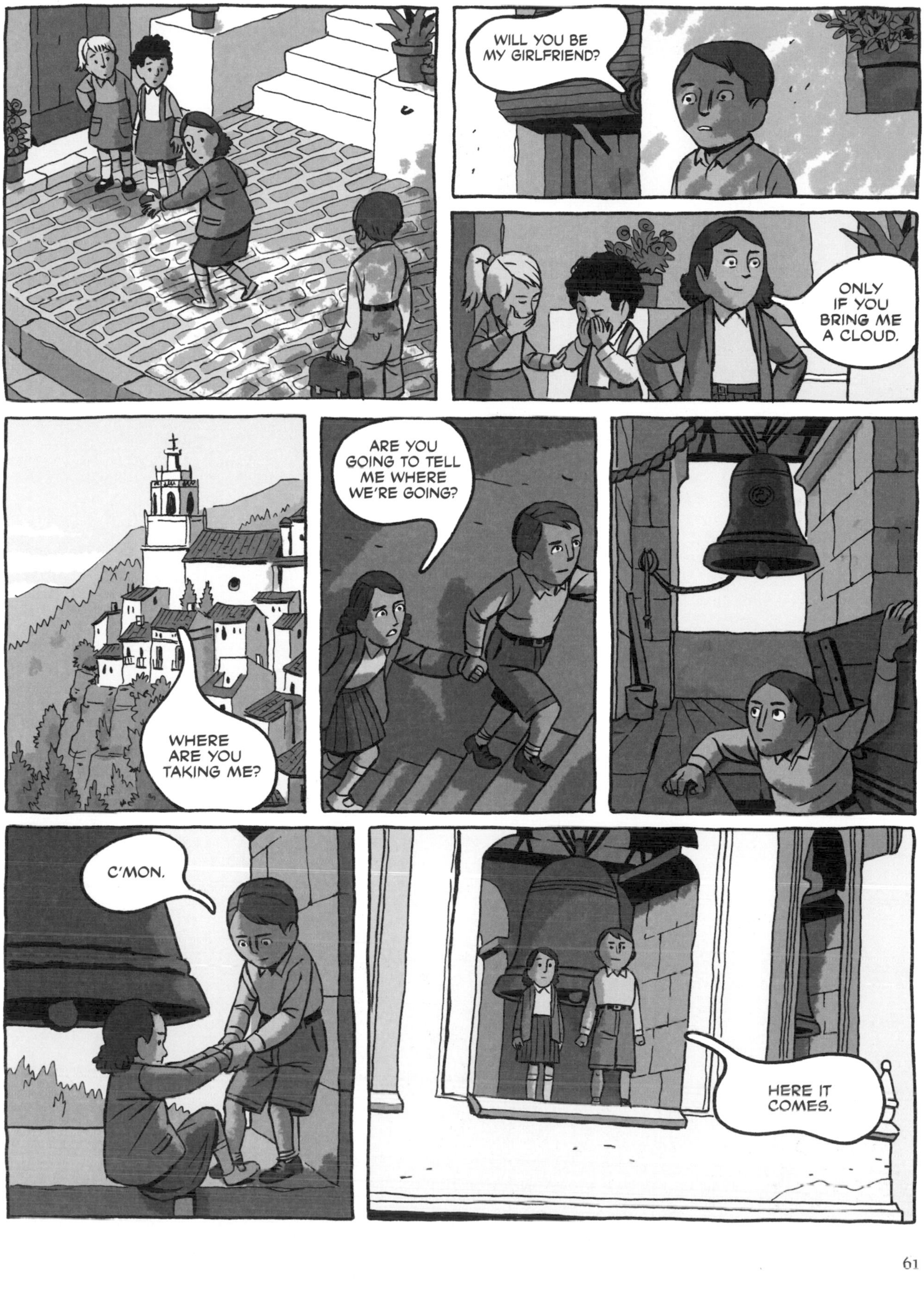
WILL YOU BE MY GIRLFRIEND?
ONLY IF YOU BRING ME A CLOUD.
WHERE ARE YOU TAKING ME?
ARE YOU GOING TO TELL ME WHERE WE'RE GOING?
C'MON.
HERE IT COMES.

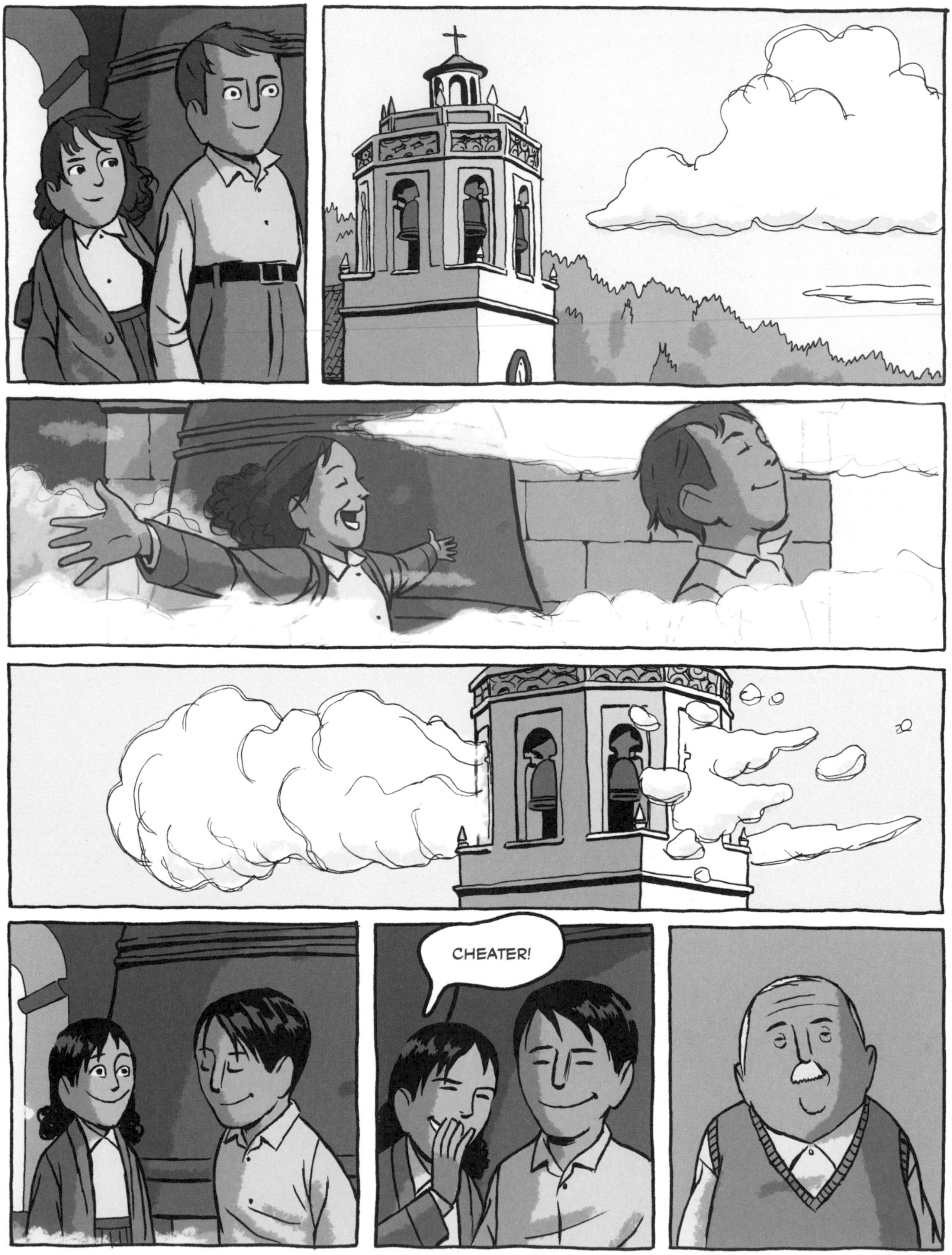
CHEATER!

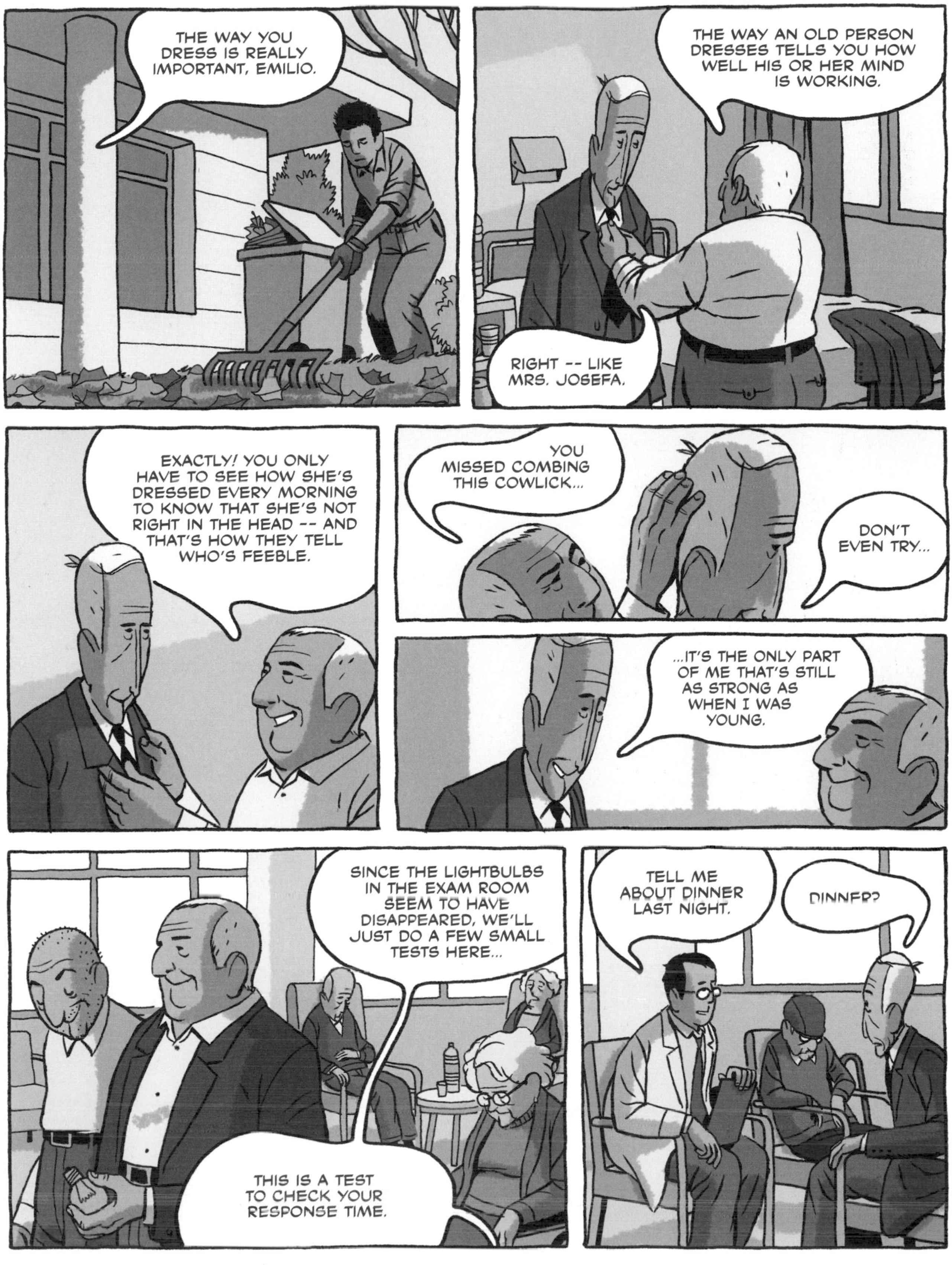

THE WAY YOU DRESS IS REALLY IMPORTANT, EMILIO.
THE WAY AN OLD PERSON DRESSES TELLS YOU HOW WELL HIS OR HER MIND IS WORKING.
RIGHT -- LIKE MRS. JOSEFA.
EXACTLY! YOU ONLY HAVE TO SEE HOW SHE'S DRESSED EVERY MORNING TO KNOW THAT SHE'S NOT RIGHT IN THE HEAD -- AND THAT'S HOW THEY TELL WHO'S FEEBLE.
YOU MISSED COMBING THIS COWLICK...
DON'T EVEN TRY...
...IT'S THE ONLY PART OF ME THAT'S STILL AS STRONG AS WHEN I WAS YOUNG.
SINCE THE LIGHTBULBS IN THE EXAM ROOM SEEM TO HAVE DISAPPEARED, WE'LL JUST DO A FEW SMALL TESTS HERE...
THIS IS A TEST TO CHECK YOUR RESPONSE TIME.
TELL ME ABOUT DINNER LAST NIGHT.
DINNER?

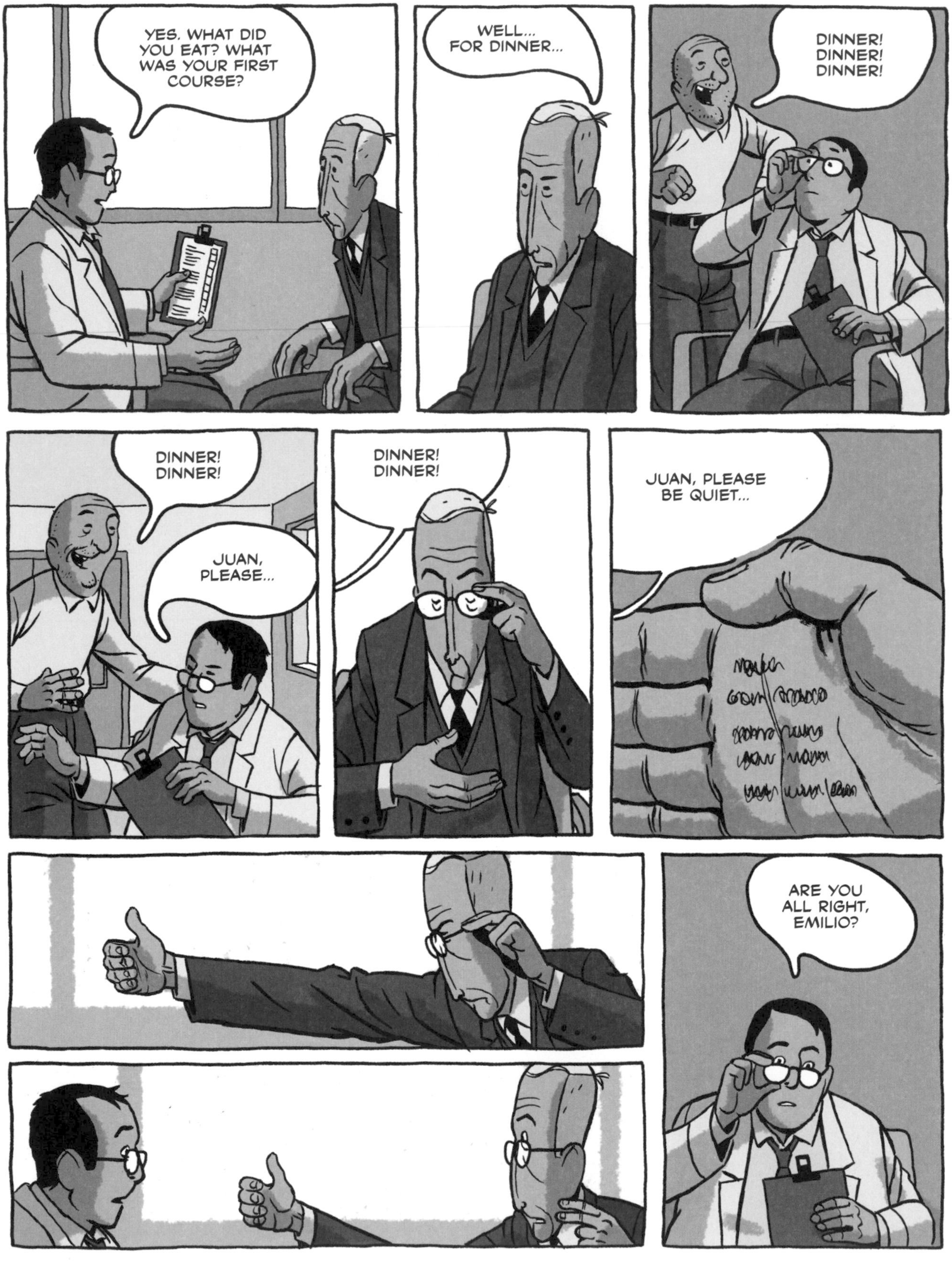
YES. WHAT DID YOU EAT? WHAT WAS YOUR FIRST COURSE?
WELL... FOR DINNER...
DINNER! DINNER! DINNER!
DINNER! DINNER!
JUAN, PLEASE...
DINNER! DINNER!
JUAN, PLEASE BE QUIET...
ARE YOU ALL RIGHT, EMILIO?

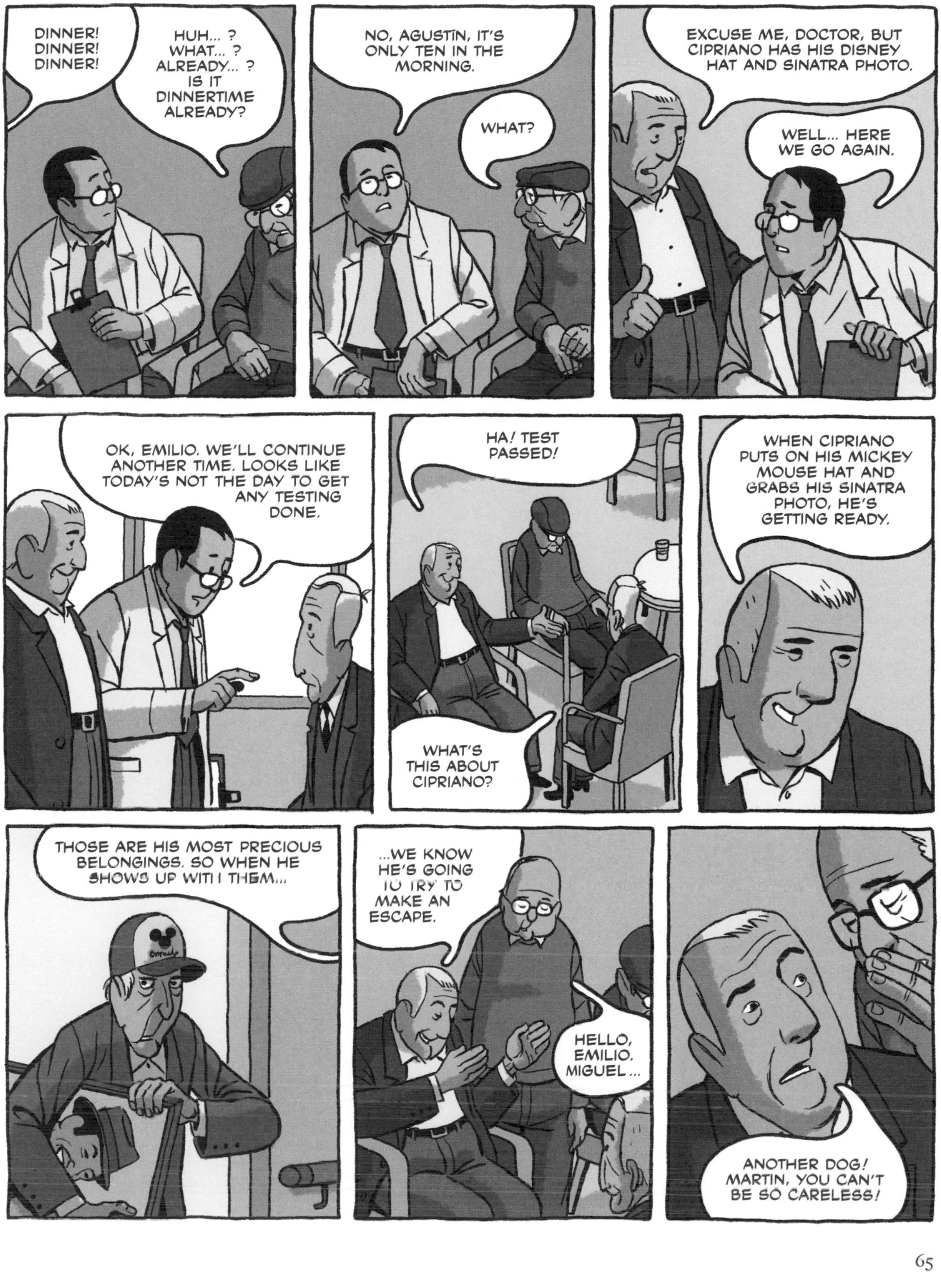
DINNER! DINNER! DINNER!
HUH... ? WHAT... ? ALREADY... ? IS IT DINNERTIME ALREADY?
NO, AGUSTÍN, IT'S ONLY TEN IN THE MORNING.
WHAT?
EXCUSE ME, DOCTOR, BUT CIPRIANO HAS HIS DISNEY HAT AND SINATRA PHOTO.
WELL... HERE WE GO AGAIN.
OK, EMILIO. WE'LL CONTINUE ANOTHER TIME. LOOKS LIKE TODAY'S NOT THE DAY TO GET ANY TESTING DONE.
HA! TEST PASSED!
WHAT'S THIS ABOUT CIPRIANO?
WHEN CIPRIANO PUTS ON HIS MICKEY MOUSE HAT AND GRABS HIS SINATRA PHOTO, HE'S GETTING READY.
THOSE ARE HIS MOST PRECIOUS BELONGINGS. SO WHEN HE SHOWS UP WITH THEM...
...WE KNOW HE'S GOING TO TRY TO MAKE AN ESCAPE.
HELLO, EMILIO. MIGUEL...
ANOTHER DOG! MARTIN, YOU CAN'T BE SO CARELESS!

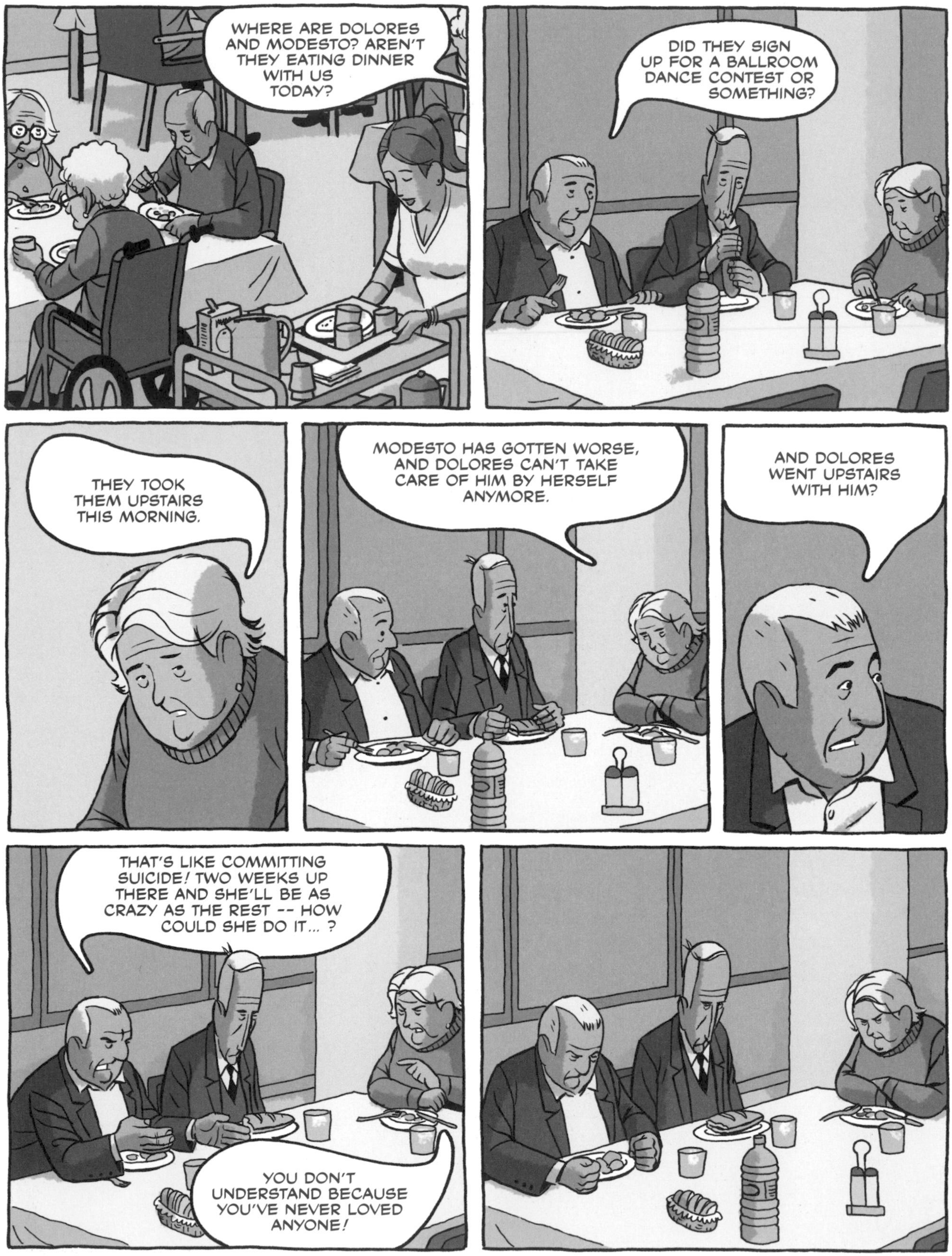
WHERE ARE DOLORES AND MODESTO? AREN'T THEY EATING DINNER WITH US TODAY?
DID THEY SIGN UP FOR A BALLROOM DANCE CONTEST OR SOMETHING?
THEY TOOK THEM UPSTAIRS THIS MORNING.
MODESTO HAS GOTTEN WORSE, AND DOLORES CAN'T TAKE CARE OF HIM BY HERSELF ANYMORE.
AND DOLORES WENT UPSTAIRS WITH HIM?
THAT'S LIKE COMMITTING SUICIDE! TWO WEEKS UP THERE AND SHE'LL BE AS CRAZY AS THE REST -- HOW COULD SHE DO IT... ?
YOU DON'T UNDERSTAND BECAUSE YOU'VE NEVER LOVED ANYONE!

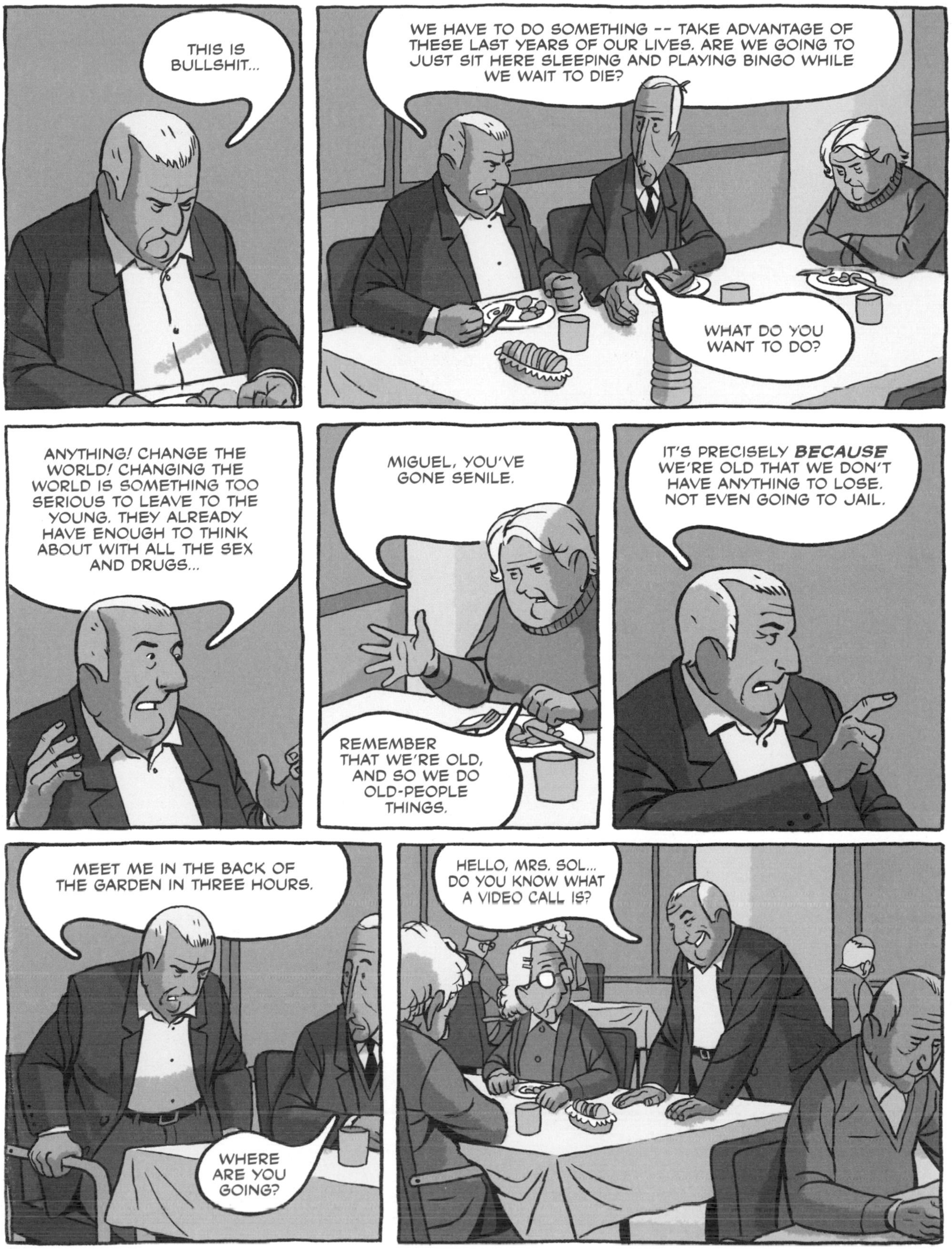
THIS IS BULLSHIT...
WE HAVE TO DO SOMETHING -- TAKE ADVANTAGE OF THESE LAST YEARS OF OUR LIVES. ARE WE GOING TO JUST SIT HERE SLEEPING AND PLAYING BINGO WHILE WE WAIT TO DIE?
WHAT DO YOU WANT TO DO?
ANYTHING! CHANGE THE WORLD! CHANGING THE WORLD IS SOMETHING TOO SERIOUS TO LEAVE TO THE YOUNG. THEY ALREADY HAVE ENOUGH TO THINK ABOUT WITH ALL THE SEX AND DRUGS...
MIGUEL, YOU'VE GONE SENILE.
REMEMBER THAT WE'RE OLD, AND SO WE DO OLD-PEOPLE THINGS.
IT'S PRECISELY *BECAUSE* WE'RE OLD THAT WE DON'T HAVE ANYTHING TO LOSE. NOT EVEN GOING TO JAIL.
MEET ME IN THE BACK OF THE GARDEN IN THREE HOURS.
WHERE ARE YOU GOING?
HELLO, MRS. SOL... DO YOU KNOW WHAT A VIDEO CALL IS?

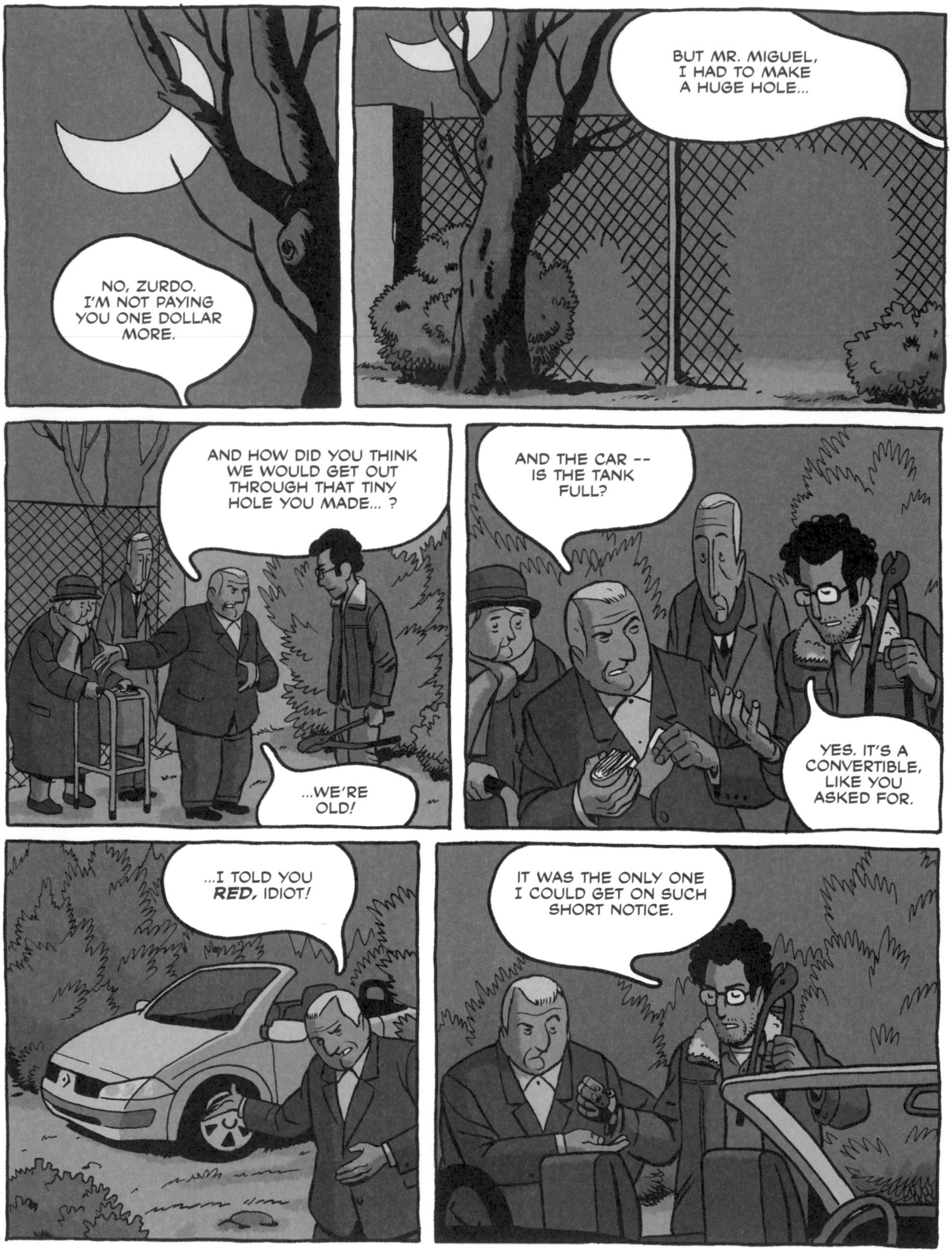
NO, ZURDO. I'M NOT PAYING YOU ONE DOLLAR MORE.
BUT MR. MIGUEL, I HAD TO MAKE A HUGE HOLE...
AND HOW DID YOU THINK WE WOULD GET OUT THROUGH THAT TINY HOLE YOU MADE... ?
...WE'RE OLD!
AND THE CAR -- IS THE TANK FULL?
YES. IT'S A CONVERTIBLE, LIKE YOU ASKED FOR.
...I TOLD YOU **RED,** IDIOT!
IT WAS THE ONLY ONE I COULD GET ON SUCH SHORT NOTICE.

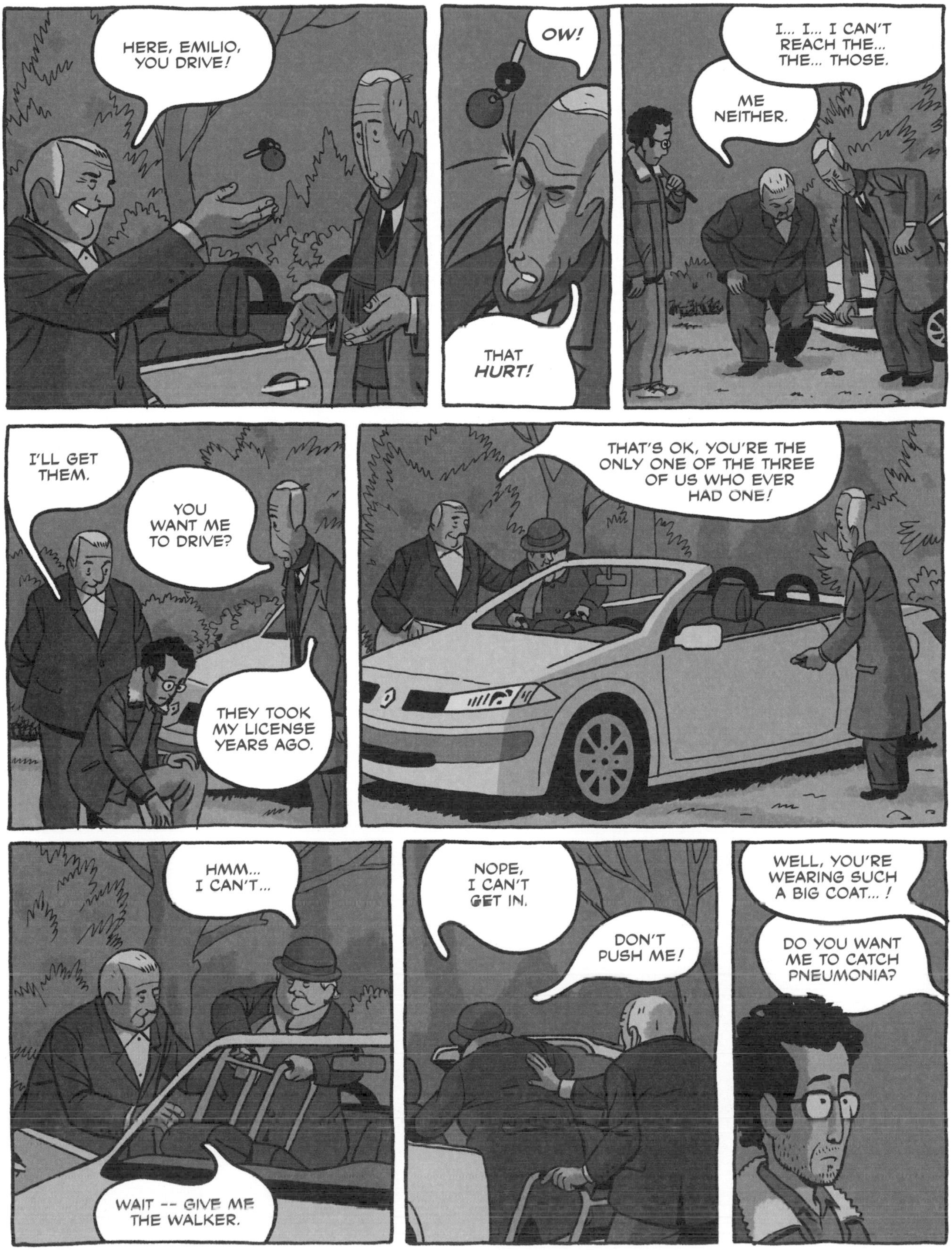
HERE, EMILIO, YOU DRIVE!
OW!
THAT HURT!
I... I... I CAN'T REACH THE... THE... THOSE.
ME NEITHER.
I'LL GET THEM.
YOU WANT ME TO DRIVE?
THEY TOOK MY LICENSE YEARS AGO.
THAT'S OK, YOU'RE THE ONLY ONE OF THE THREE OF US WHO EVER HAD ONE!
HMM... I CAN'T...
WAIT -- GIVE ME THE WALKER.
NOPE, I CAN'T GET IN.
DON'T PUSH ME!
WELL, YOU'RE WEARING SUCH A BIG COAT... !
DO YOU WANT ME TO CATCH PNEUMONIA?

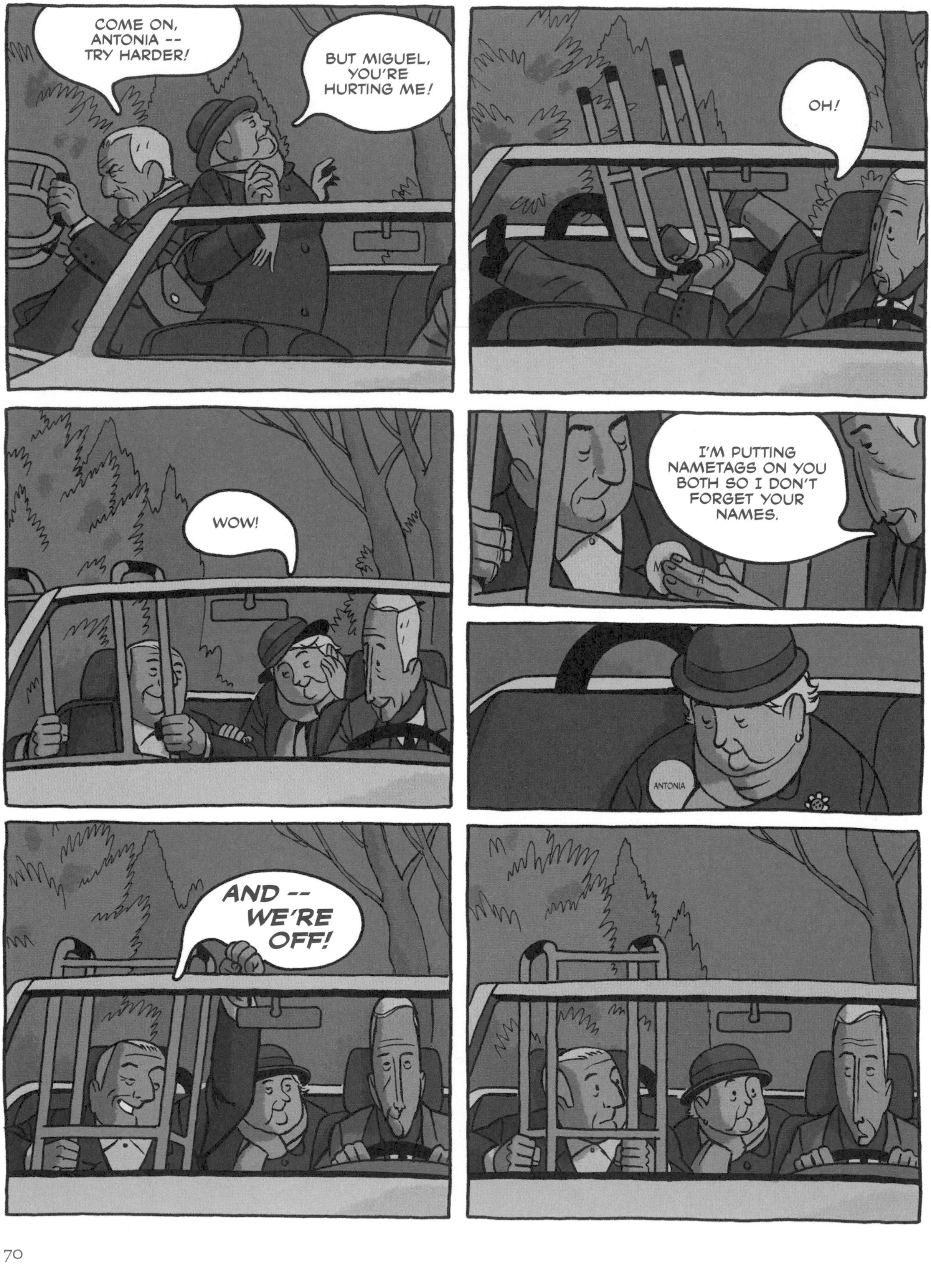
COME ON, ANTONIA -- TRY HARDER!
BUT MIGUEL, YOU'RE HURTING ME!
OH!
WOW!
I'M PUTTING NAMETAGS ON YOU BOTH SO I DON'T FORGET YOUR NAMES.
ANTONIA
AND -- WE'RE OFF!

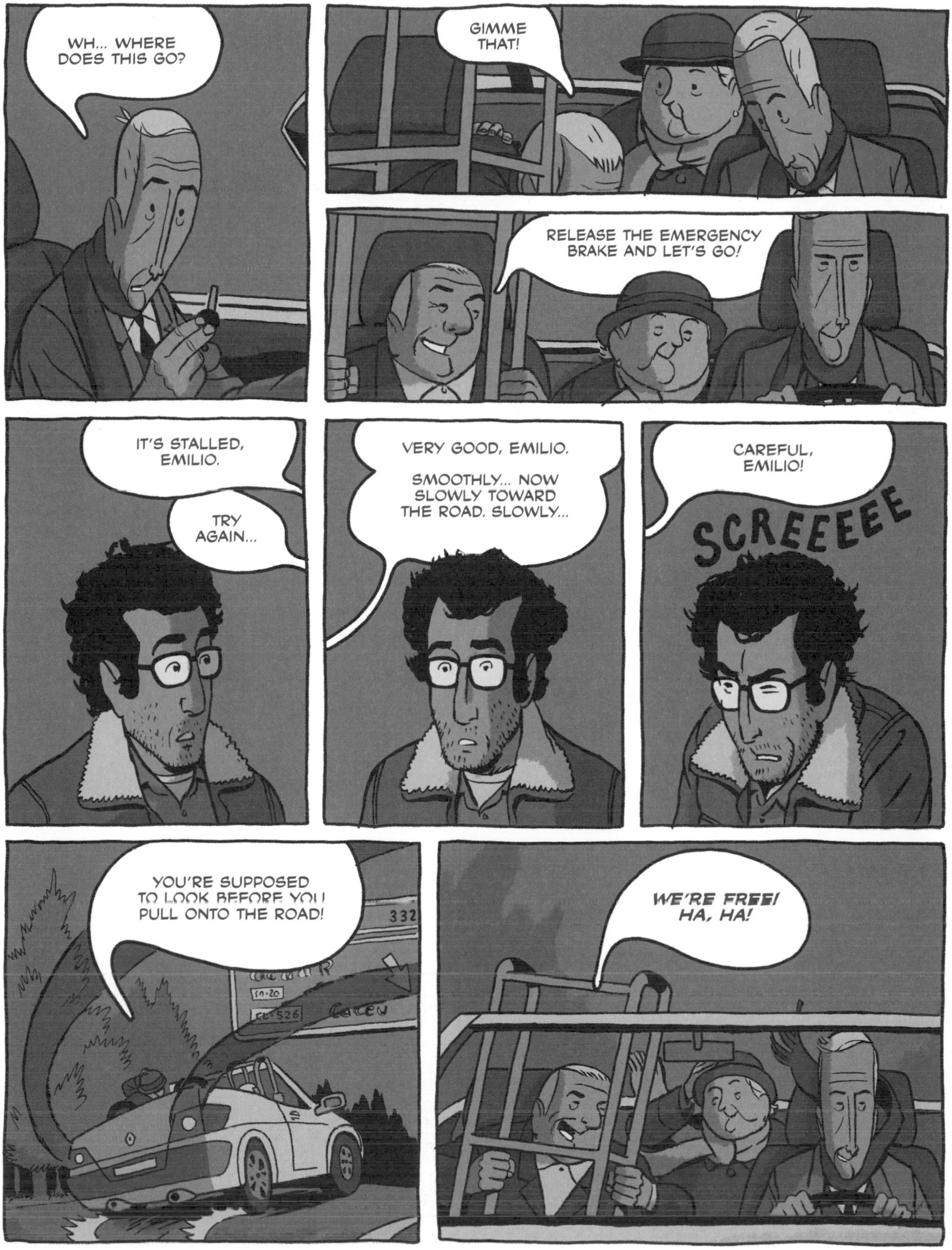
WH... WHERE DOES THIS GO?
GIMME THAT!
RELEASE THE EMERGENCY BRAKE AND LET'S GO!
IT'S STALLED, EMILIO.
TRY AGAIN...
VERY GOOD, EMILIO.
SMOOTHLY... NOW SLOWLY TOWARD THE ROAD. SLOWLY...
CAREFUL, EMILIO!
SCREEEEEE
YOU'RE SUPPOSED TO LOOK BEFORE YOU PULL ONTO THE ROAD!
332
WE'RE FREE! HA, HA!

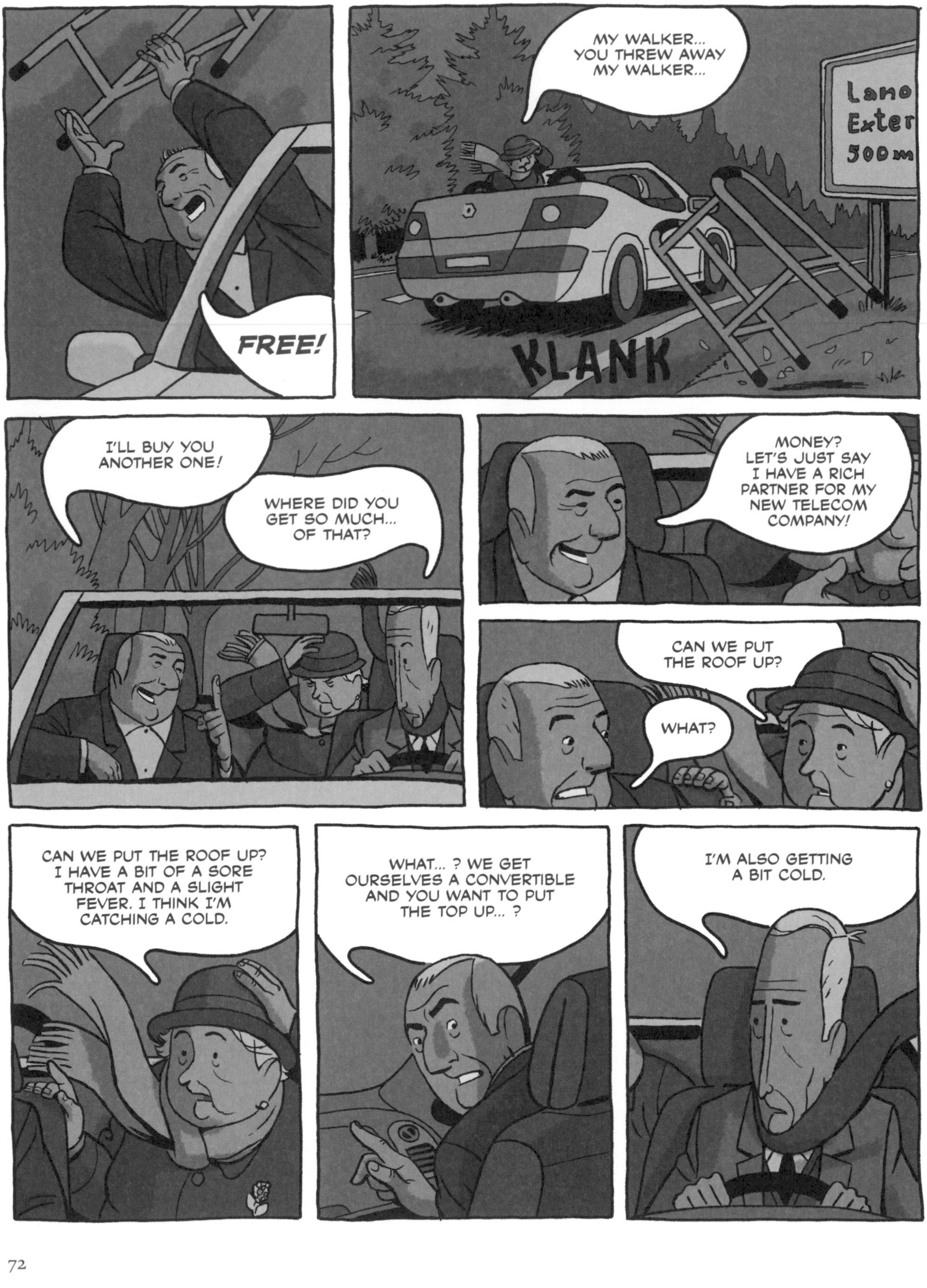
FREE!
MY WALKER... YOU THREW AWAY MY WALKER...
KLANK
I'LL BUY YOU ANOTHER ONE!
WHERE DID YOU GET SO MUCH... OF THAT?
MONEY? LET'S JUST SAY I HAVE A RICH PARTNER FOR MY NEW TELECOM COMPANY!
CAN WE PUT THE ROOF UP?
WHAT?
CAN WE PUT THE ROOF UP? I HAVE A BIT OF A SORE THROAT AND A SLIGHT FEVER. I THINK I'M CATCHING A COLD.
WHAT... ? WE GET OURSELVES A CONVERTIBLE AND YOU WANT TO PUT THE TOP UP... ?
I'M ALSO GETTING A BIT COLD.

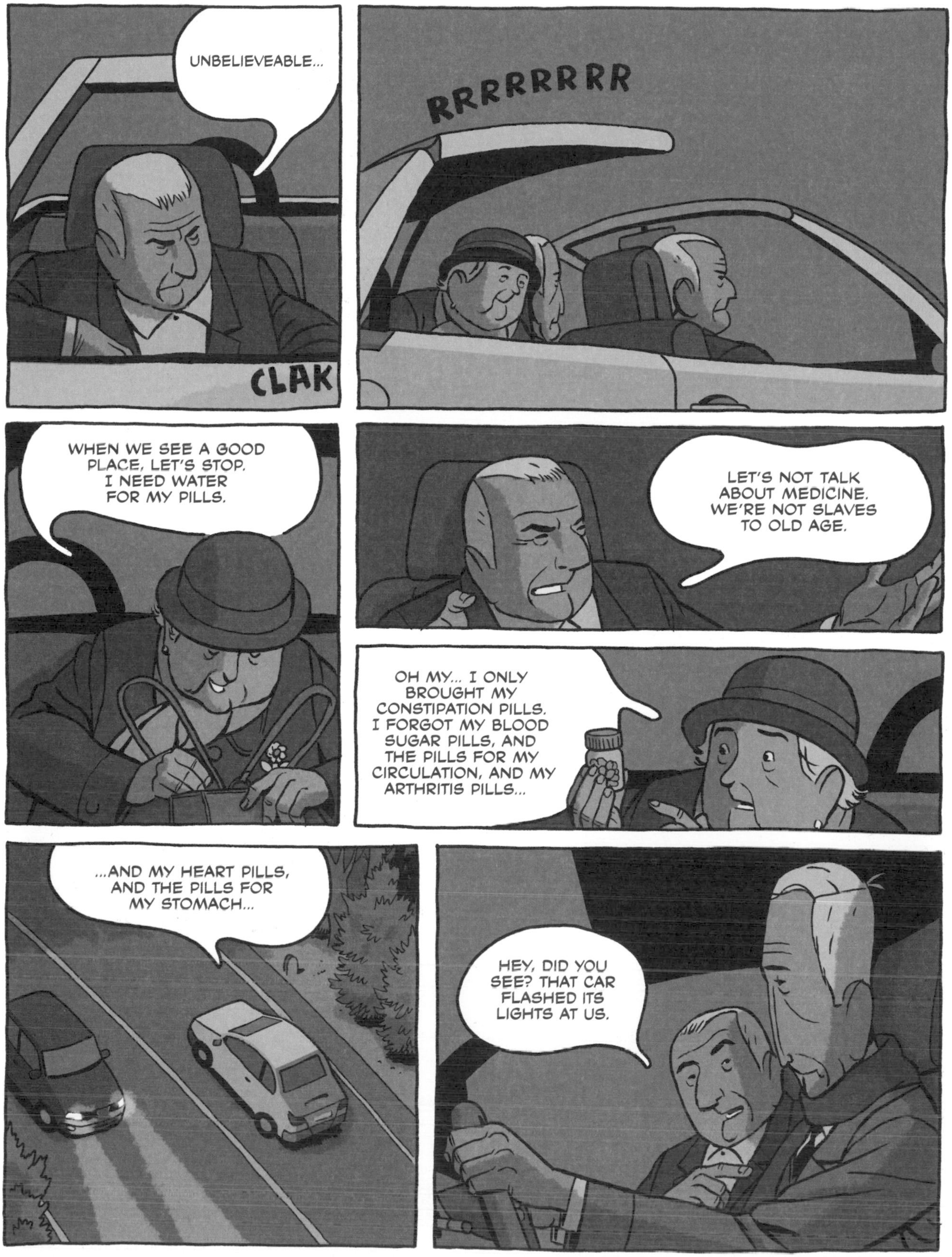
UNBELIEVEABLE...
CLAK
RRRRRRRR
WHEN WE SEE A GOOD PLACE, LET'S STOP. I NEED WATER FOR MY PILLS.
LET'S NOT TALK ABOUT MEDICINE. WE'RE NOT SLAVES TO OLD AGE.
OH MY... I ONLY BROUGHT MY CONSTIPATION PILLS. I FORGOT MY BLOOD SUGAR PILLS, AND THE PILLS FOR MY CIRCULATION, AND MY ARTHRITIS PILLS...
...AND MY HEART PILLS, AND THE PILLS FOR MY STOMACH...
HEY, DID YOU SEE? THAT CAR FLASHED ITS LIGHTS AT US.

EMILIO -- ARE OUR HEADLIGHTS ON?

I'LL GO LOOK...

CLAK

DO YOU REALIZE THAT YOU COULD HAVE BEEN KILLED?

IT'S A MIRACLE THAT ONLY ANTONIA'S ARM WAS BROKEN.

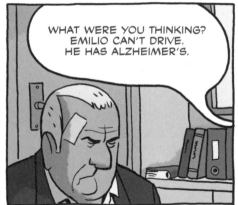

WHAT WERE YOU THINKING? EMILIO CAN'T DRIVE. HE HAS ALZHEIMER'S.

NOT TO MENTION THE MONEY YOU STOLE FROM MRS. SOL...

I DIDN'T STEAL IT! SHE *GAVE* IT TO ME.

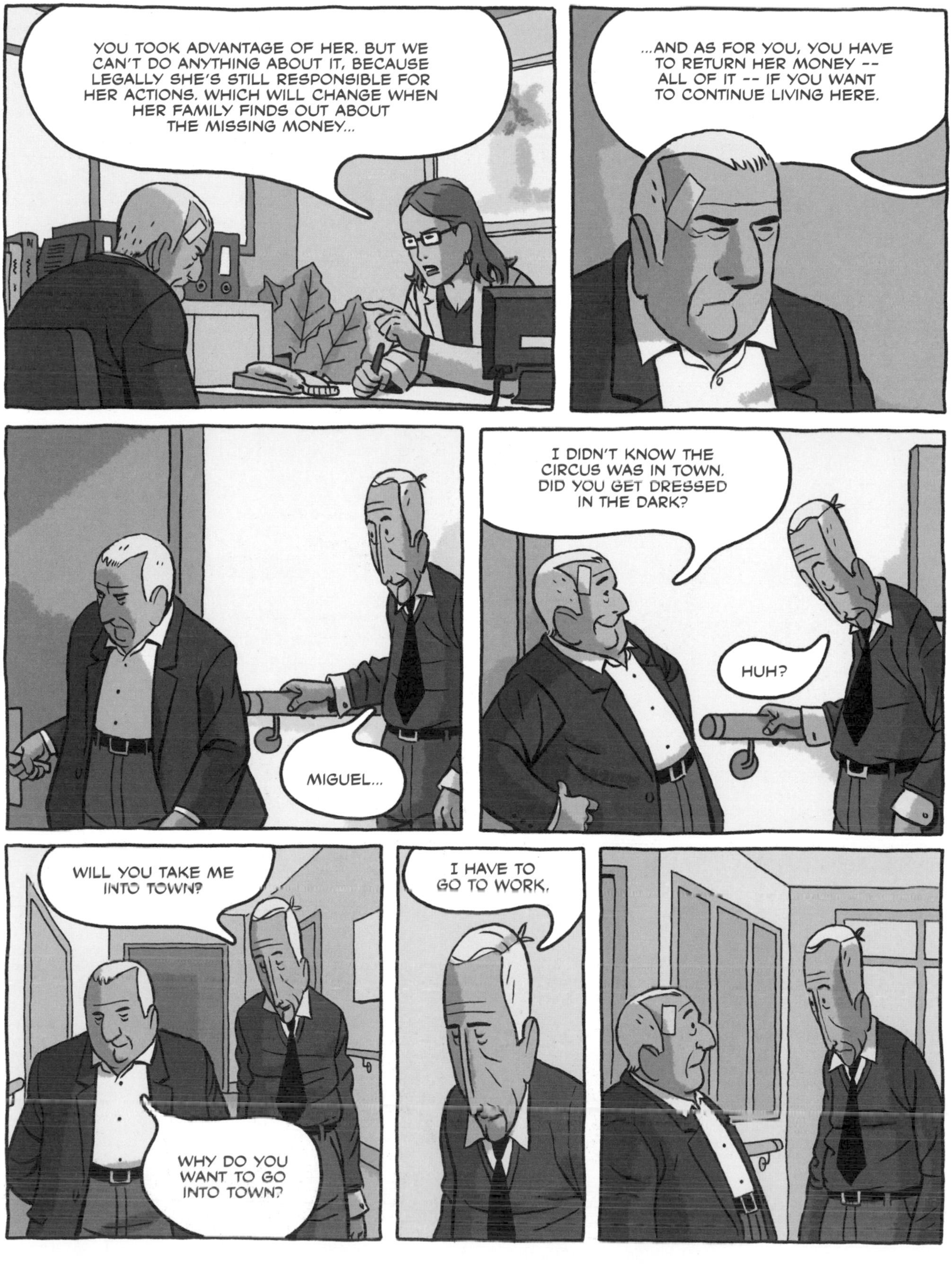
YOU TOOK ADVANTAGE OF HER. BUT WE CAN'T DO ANYTHING ABOUT IT, BECAUSE LEGALLY SHE'S STILL RESPONSIBLE FOR HER ACTIONS. WHICH WILL CHANGE WHEN HER FAMILY FINDS OUT ABOUT THE MISSING MONEY...
...AND AS FOR YOU, YOU HAVE TO RETURN HER MONEY -- ALL OF IT -- IF YOU WANT TO CONTINUE LIVING HERE.
MIGUEL...
I DIDN'T KNOW THE CIRCUS WAS IN TOWN. DID YOU GET DRESSED IN THE DARK?
HUH?
WILL YOU TAKE ME INTO TOWN?
WHY DO YOU WANT TO GO INTO TOWN?
I HAVE TO GO TO WORK.

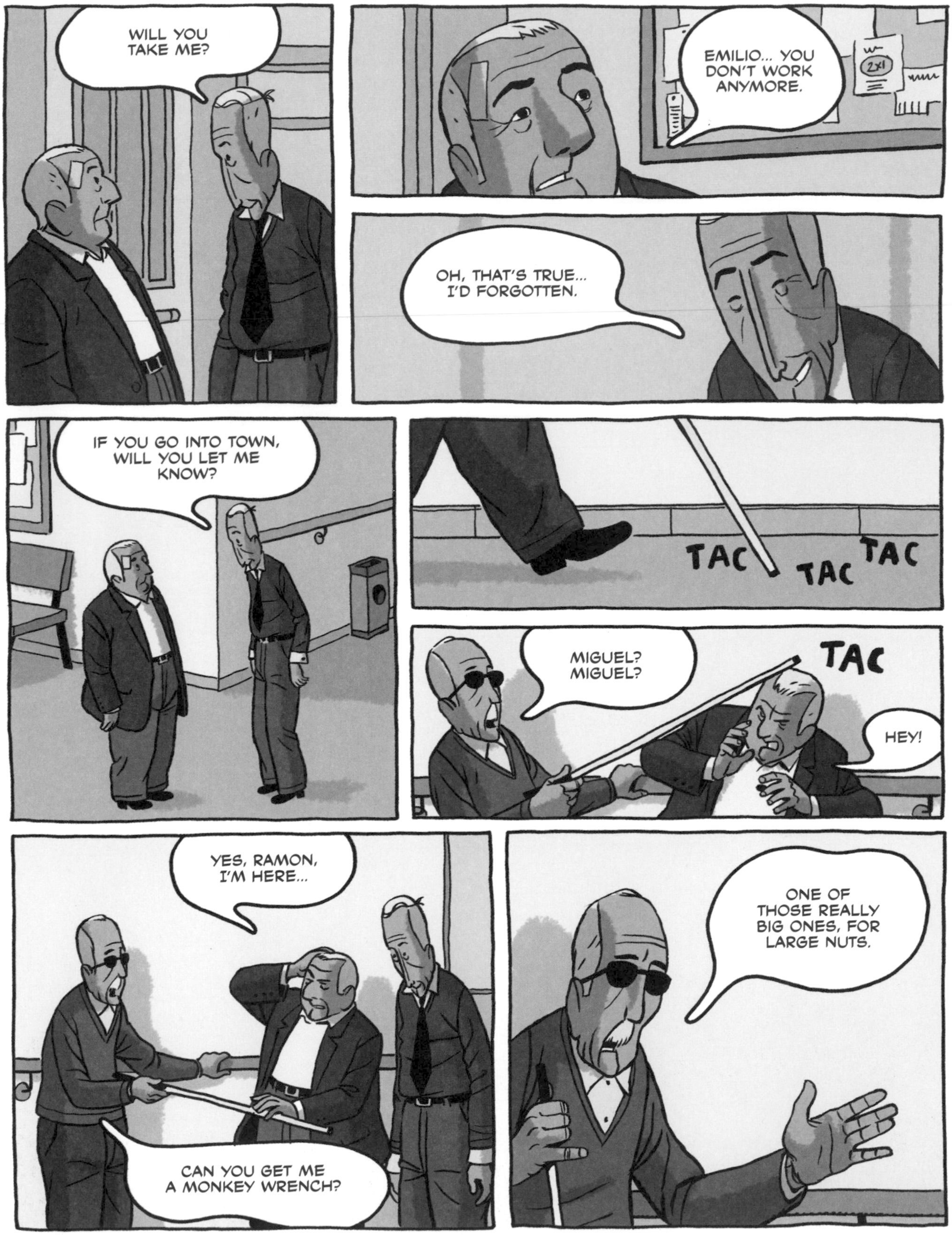
WILL YOU TAKE ME?
EMILIO... YOU DON'T WORK ANYMORE.
OH, THAT'S TRUE... I'D FORGOTTEN.
IF YOU GO INTO TOWN, WILL YOU LET ME KNOW?
TAC TAC TAC
MIGUEL? MIGUEL?
TAC
HEY!
YES, RAMON, I'M HERE...
CAN YOU GET ME A MONKEY WRENCH?
ONE OF THOSE REALLY BIG ONES, FOR LARGE NUTS.

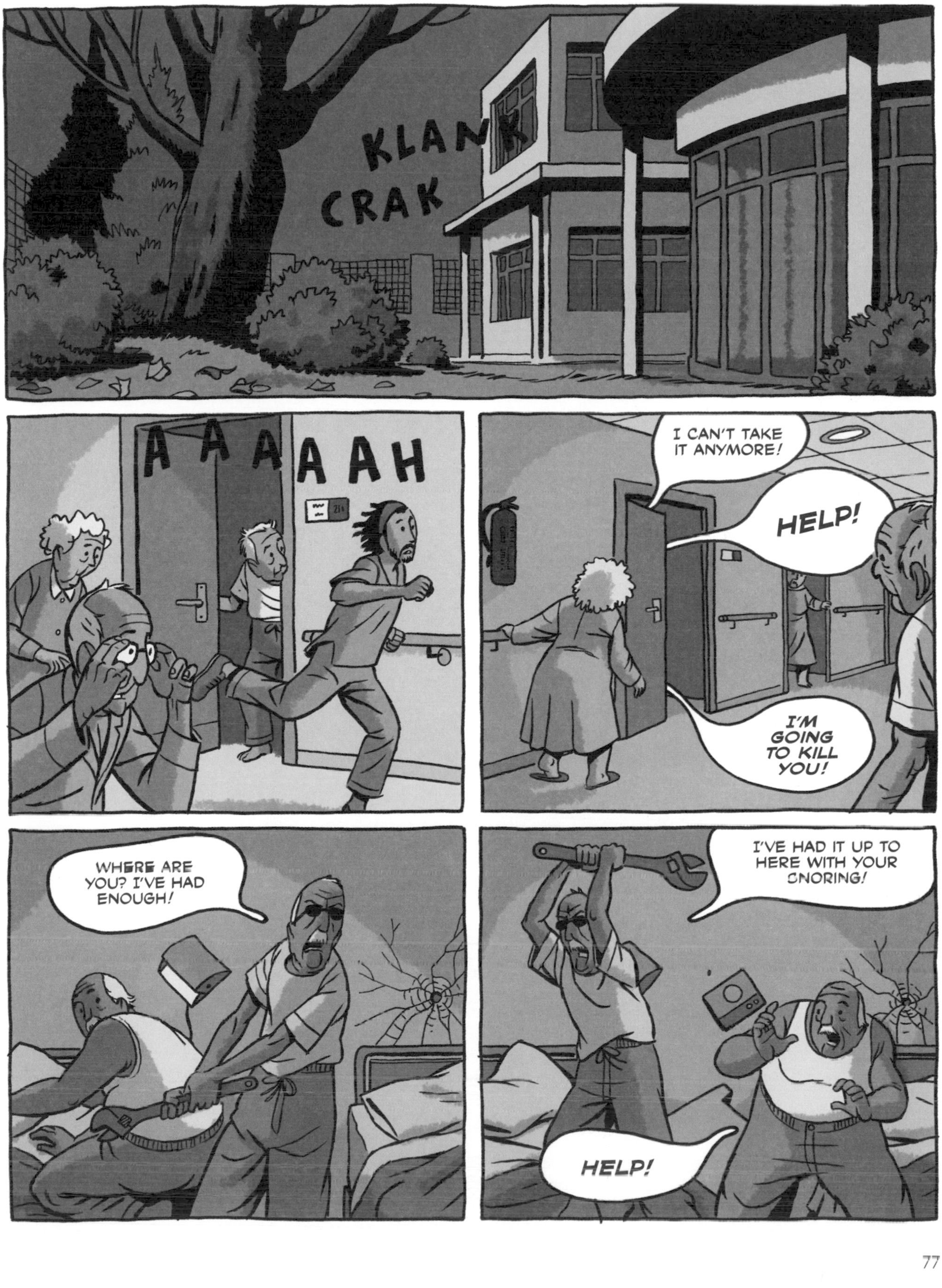
KLANK
CRAK
AAAAAH
I CAN'T TAKE IT ANYMORE!
HELP!
I'M GOING TO KILL YOU!
WHERE ARE YOU? I'VE HAD ENOUGH!
I'VE HAD IT UP TO HERE WITH YOUR SNORING!
HELP!

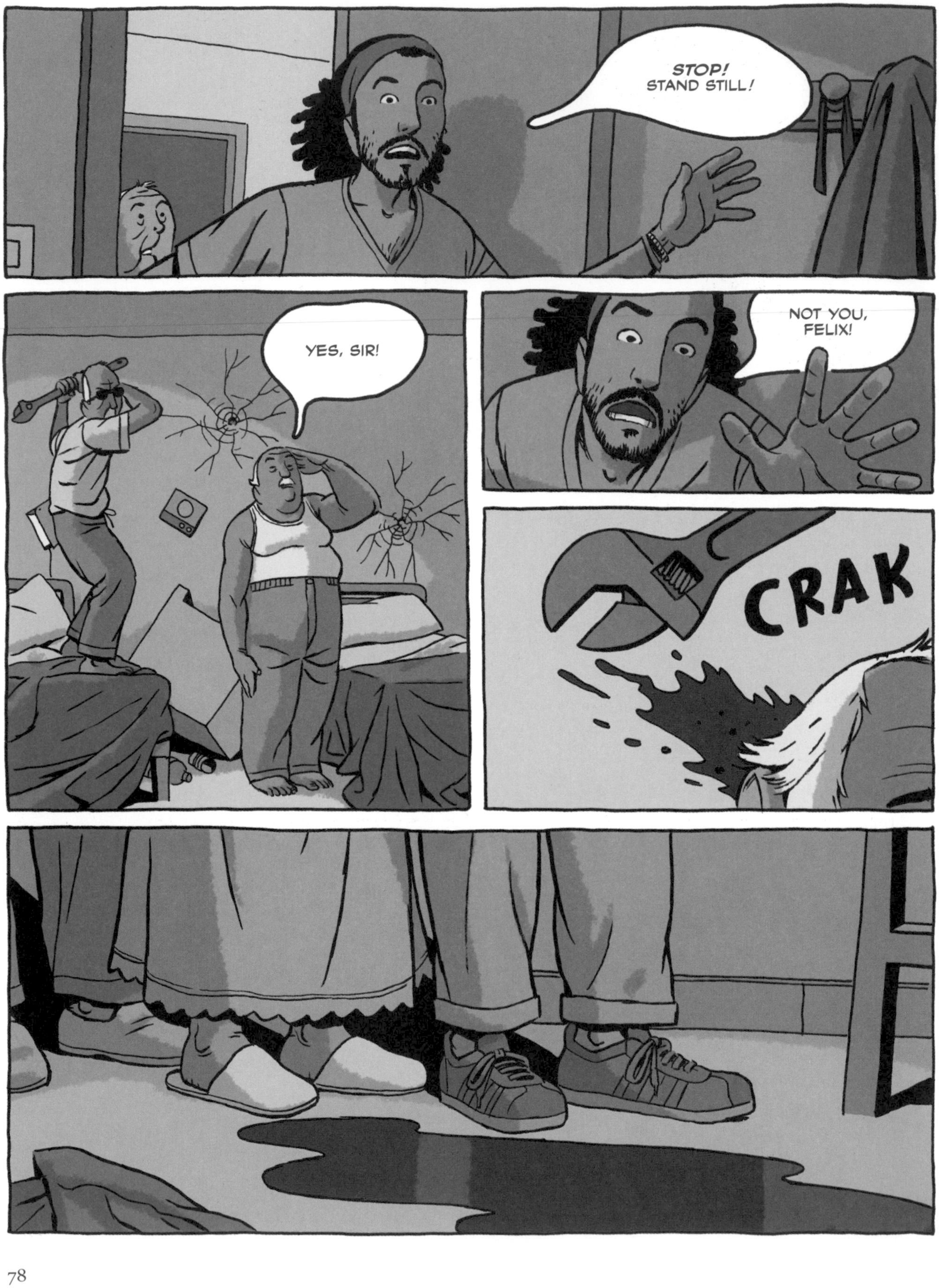
STOP!
STAND STILL!
YES, SIR!
NOT YOU,
FELIX!
CRAK

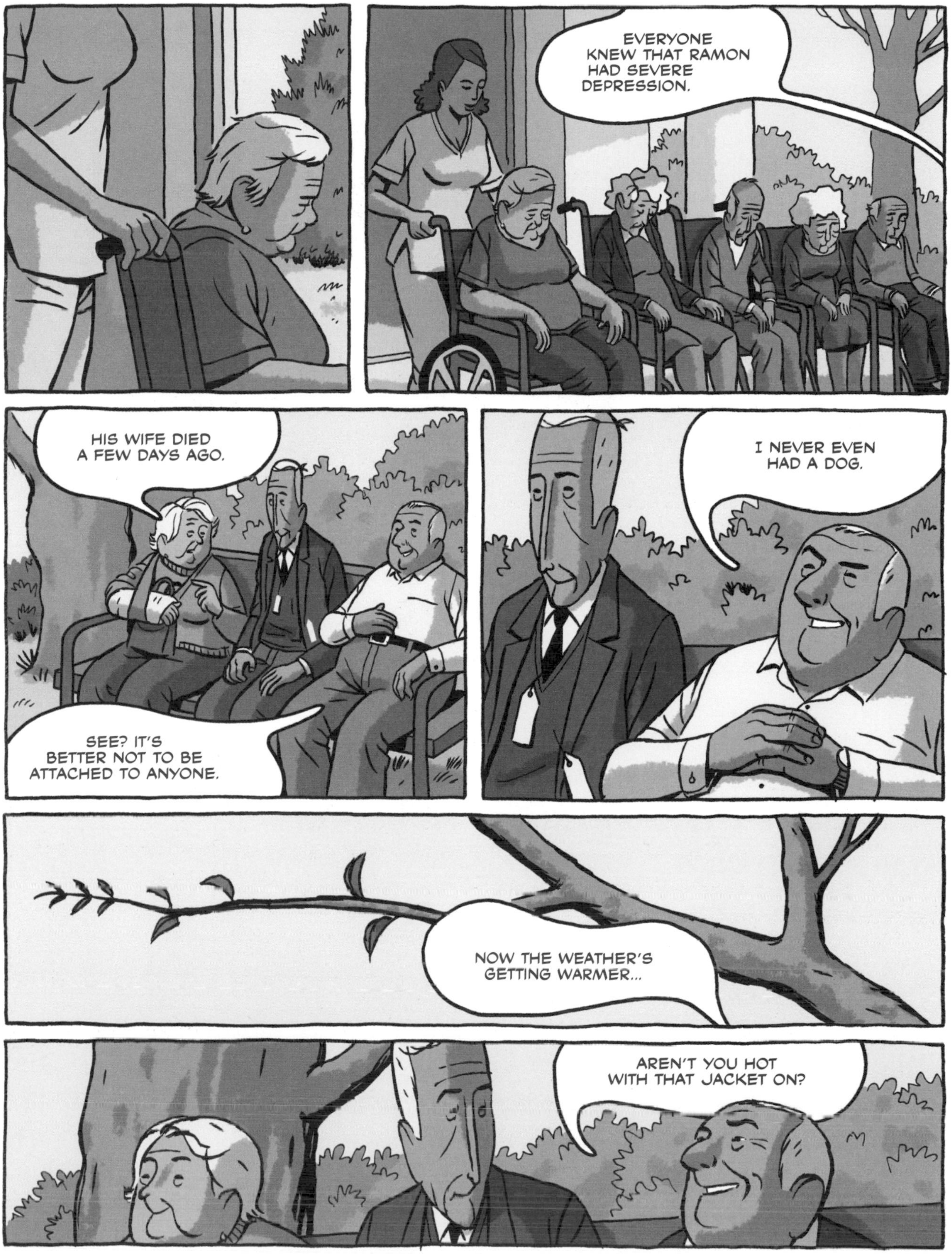
EVERYONE KNEW THAT RAMON HAD SEVERE DEPRESSION.
HIS WIFE DIED A FEW DAYS AGO.
SEE? IT'S BETTER NOT TO BE ATTACHED TO ANYONE.
I NEVER EVEN HAD A DOG.
NOW THE WEATHER'S GETTING WARMER...
AREN'T YOU HOT WITH THAT JACKET ON?

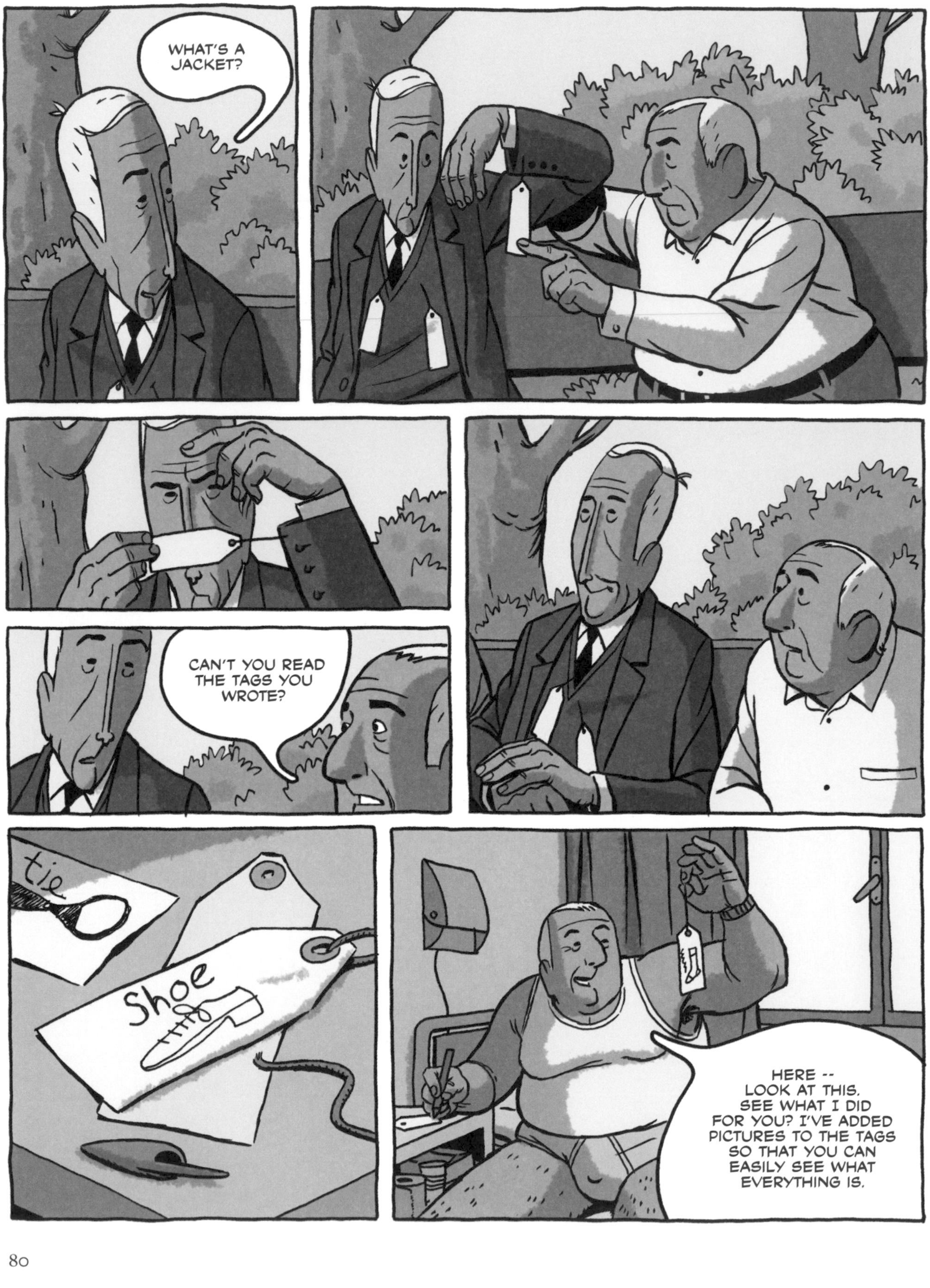
WHAT'S A JACKET?
CAN'T YOU READ THE TAGS YOU WROTE?
tie
Shoe
HERE -- LOOK AT THIS. SEE WHAT I DID FOR YOU? I'VE ADDED PICTURES TO THE TAGS SO THAT YOU CAN EASILY SEE WHAT EVERYTHING IS.

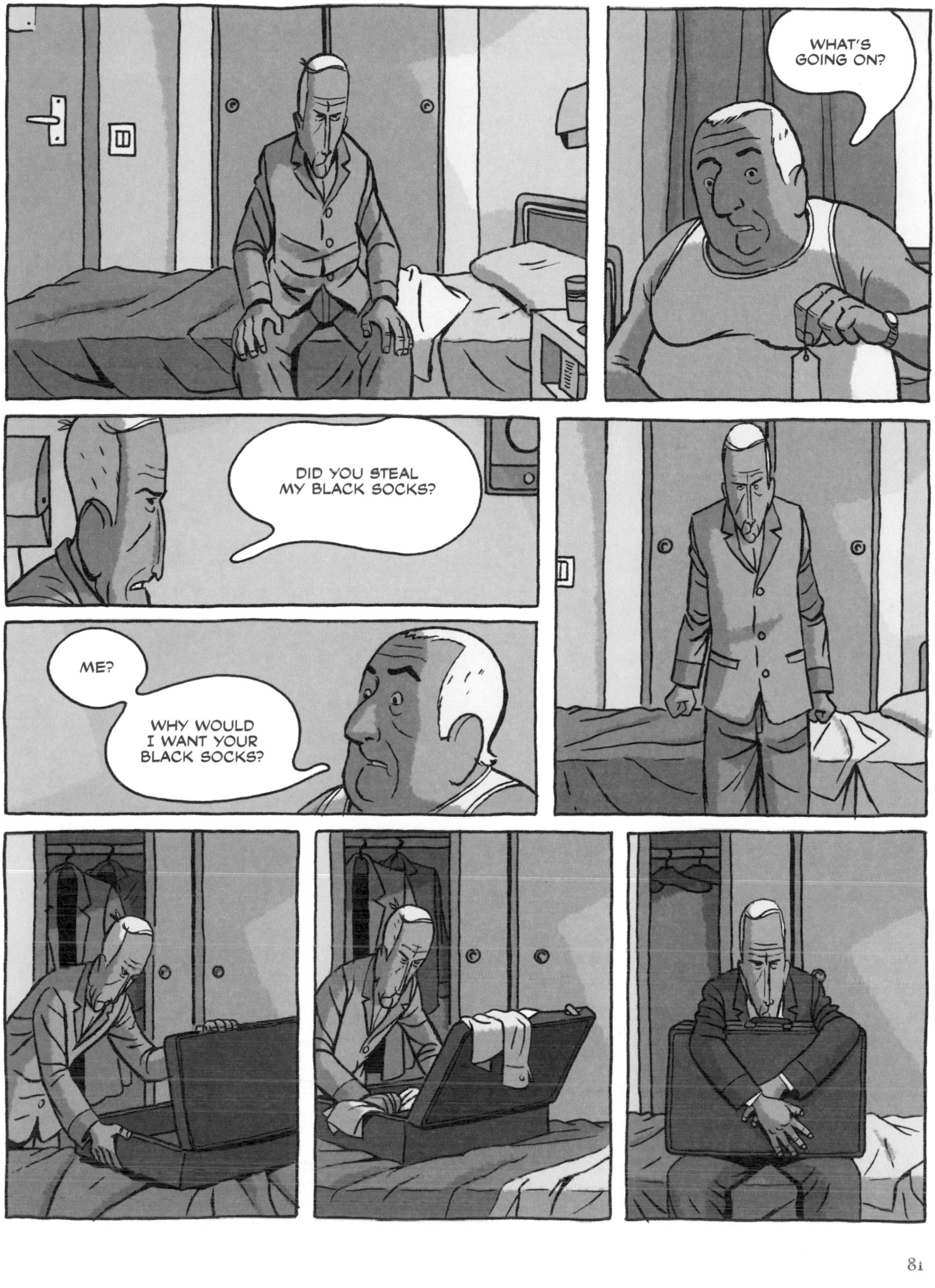
WHAT'S GOING ON?
DID YOU STEAL MY BLACK SOCKS?
ME?
WHY WOULD I WANT YOUR BLACK SOCKS?

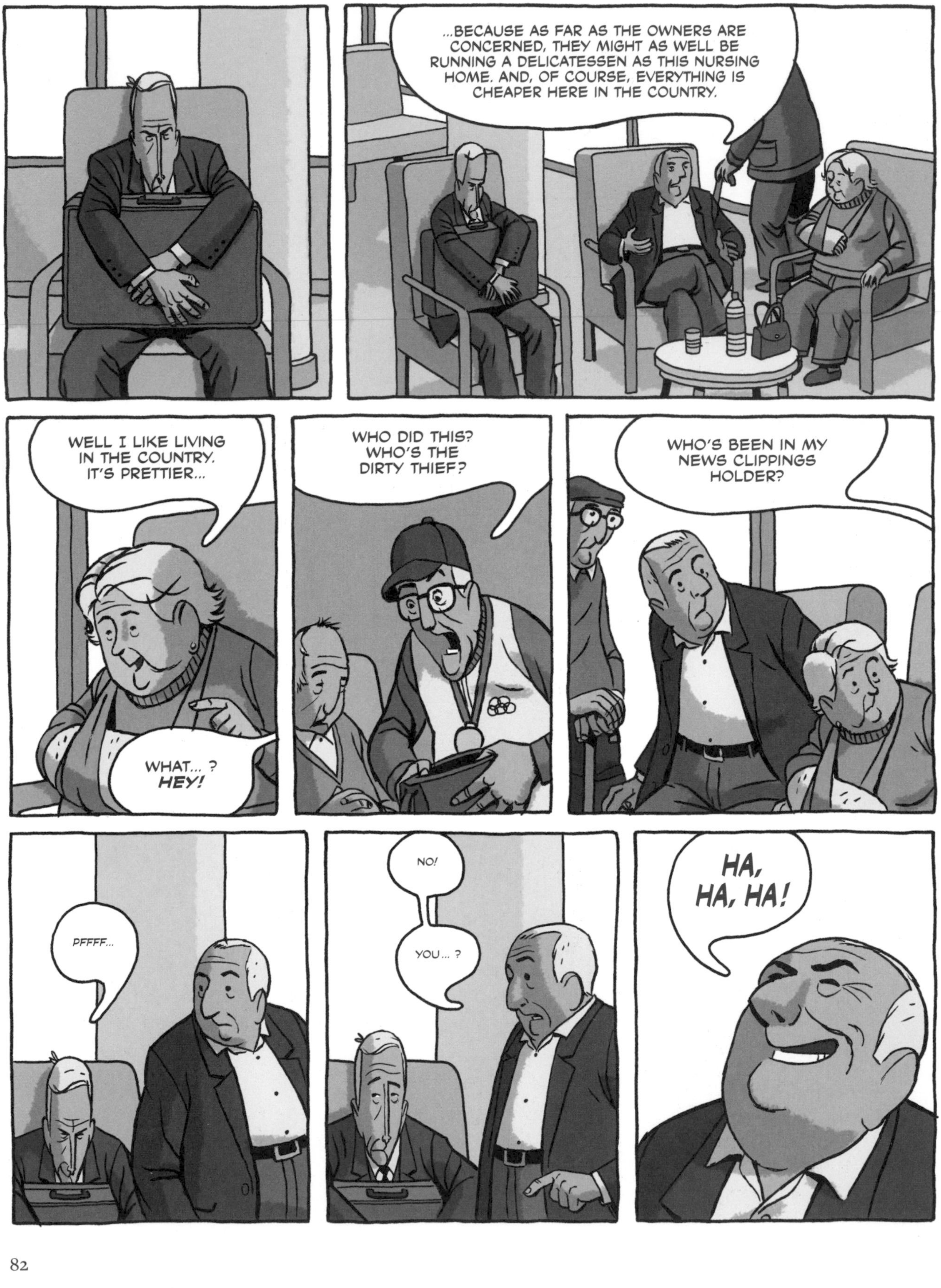
...BECAUSE AS FAR AS THE OWNERS ARE CONCERNED, THEY MIGHT AS WELL BE RUNNING A DELICATESSEN AS THIS NURSING HOME. AND, OF COURSE, EVERYTHING IS CHEAPER HERE IN THE COUNTRY.
WELL I LIKE LIVING IN THE COUNTRY. IT'S PRETTIER...
WHAT... ? HEY!
WHO DID THIS? WHO'S THE DIRTY THIEF?
WHO'S BEEN IN MY NEWS CLIPPINGS HOLDER?
PFFFF...
NO!
YOU... ?
HA, HA, HA!

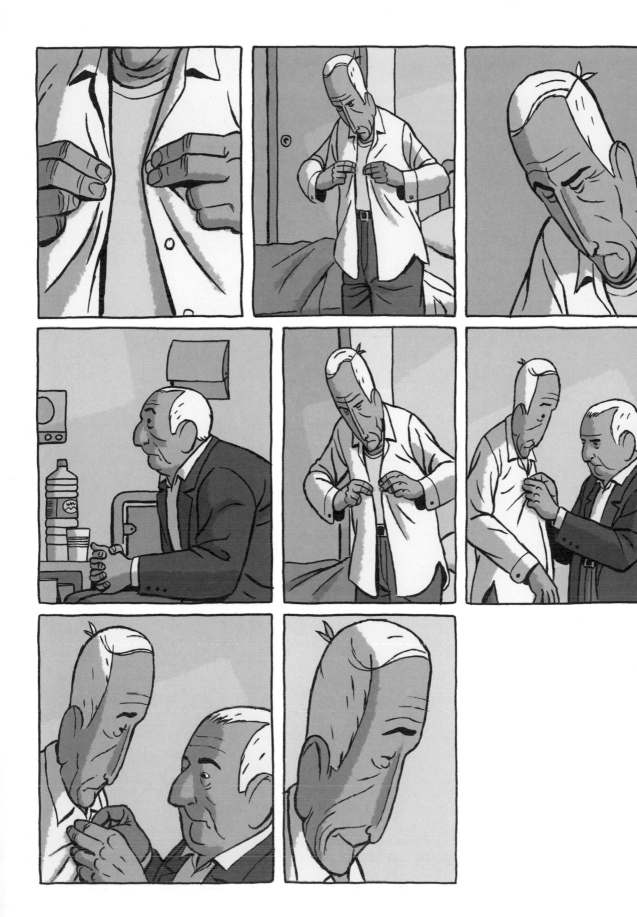

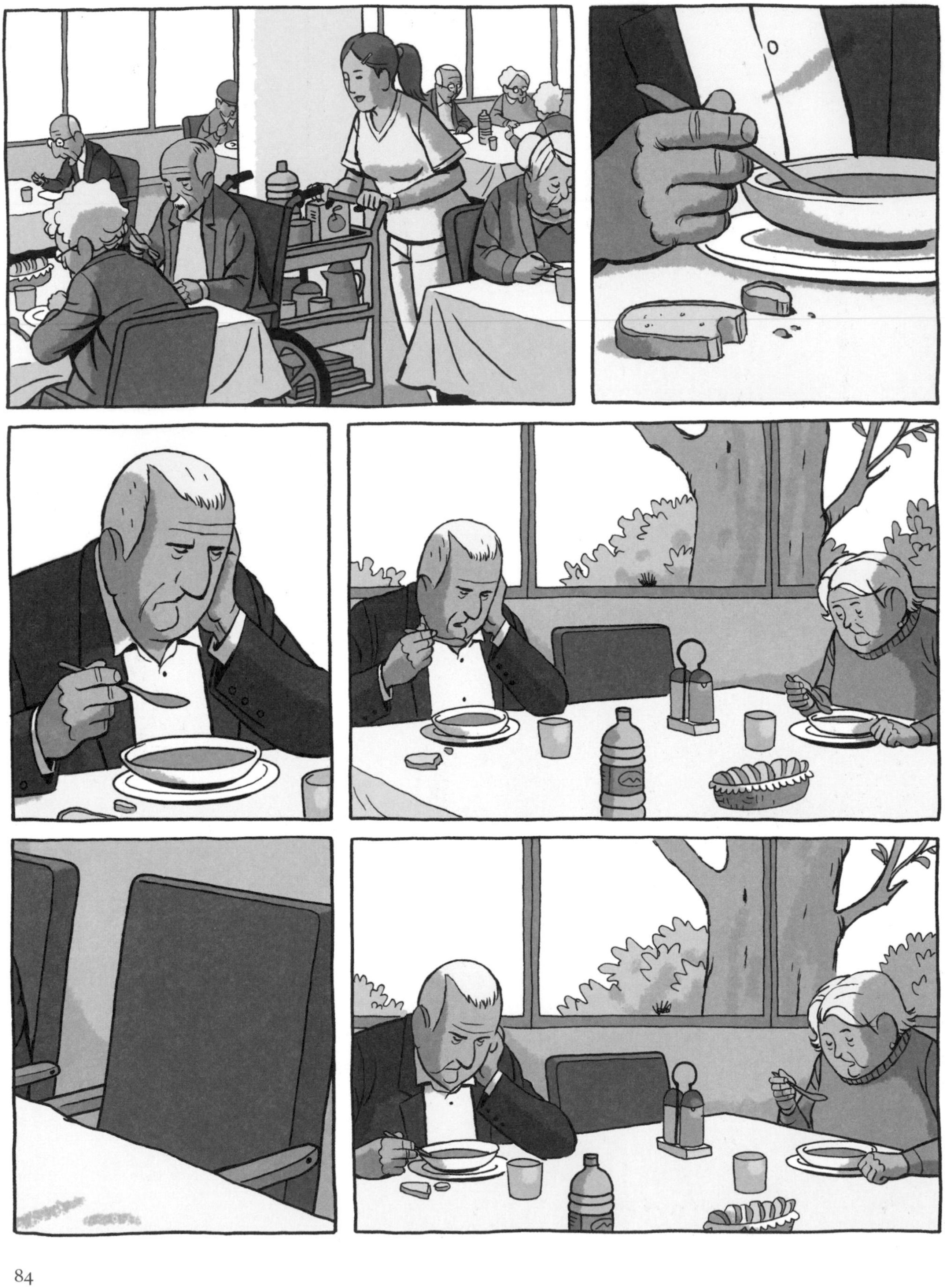

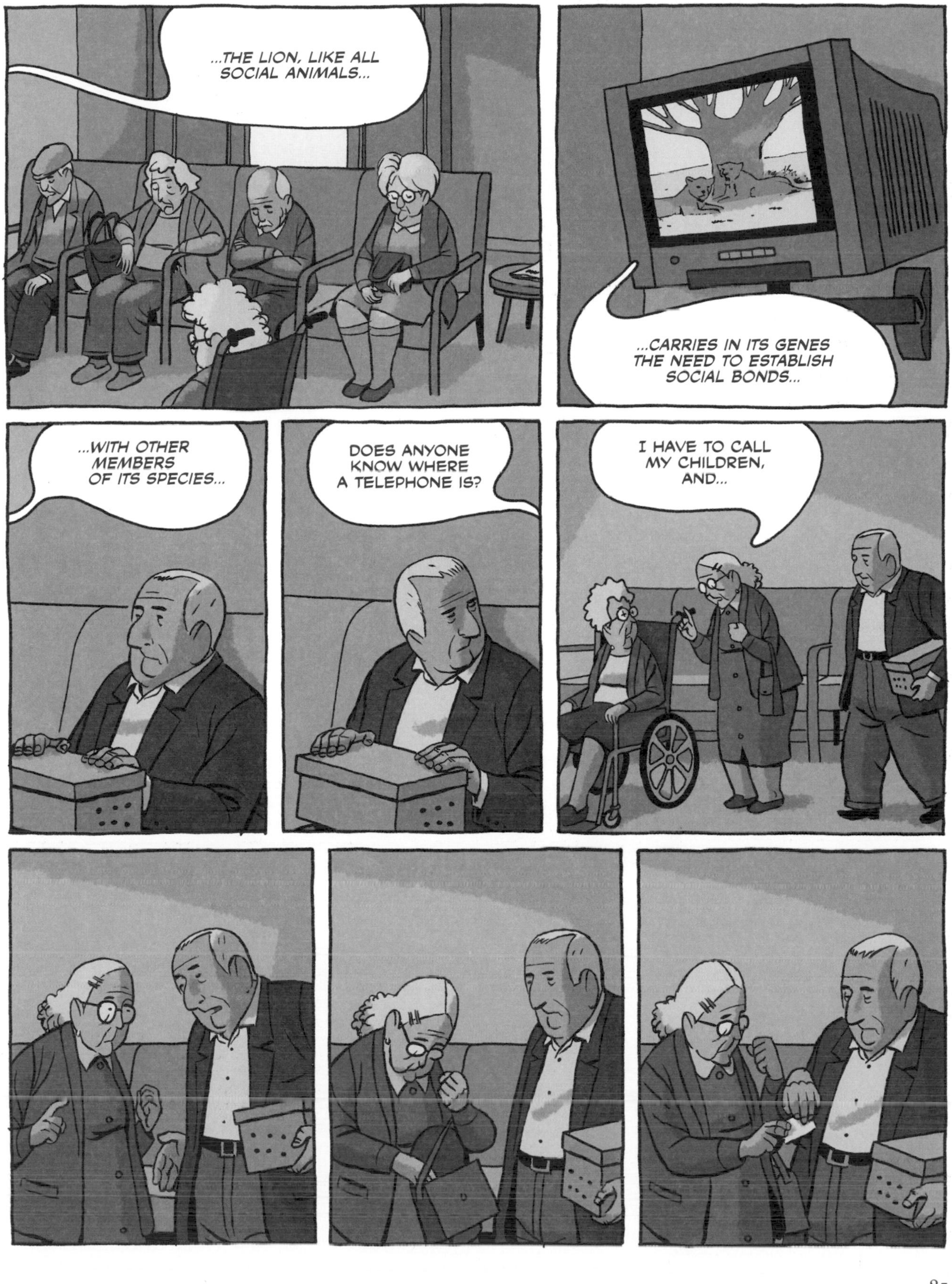
...THE LION, LIKE ALL SOCIAL ANIMALS...
...CARRIES IN ITS GENES THE NEED TO ESTABLISH SOCIAL BONDS...
...WITH OTHER MEMBERS OF ITS SPECIES...
DOES ANYONE KNOW WHERE A TELEPHONE IS?
I HAVE TO CALL MY CHILDREN, AND...

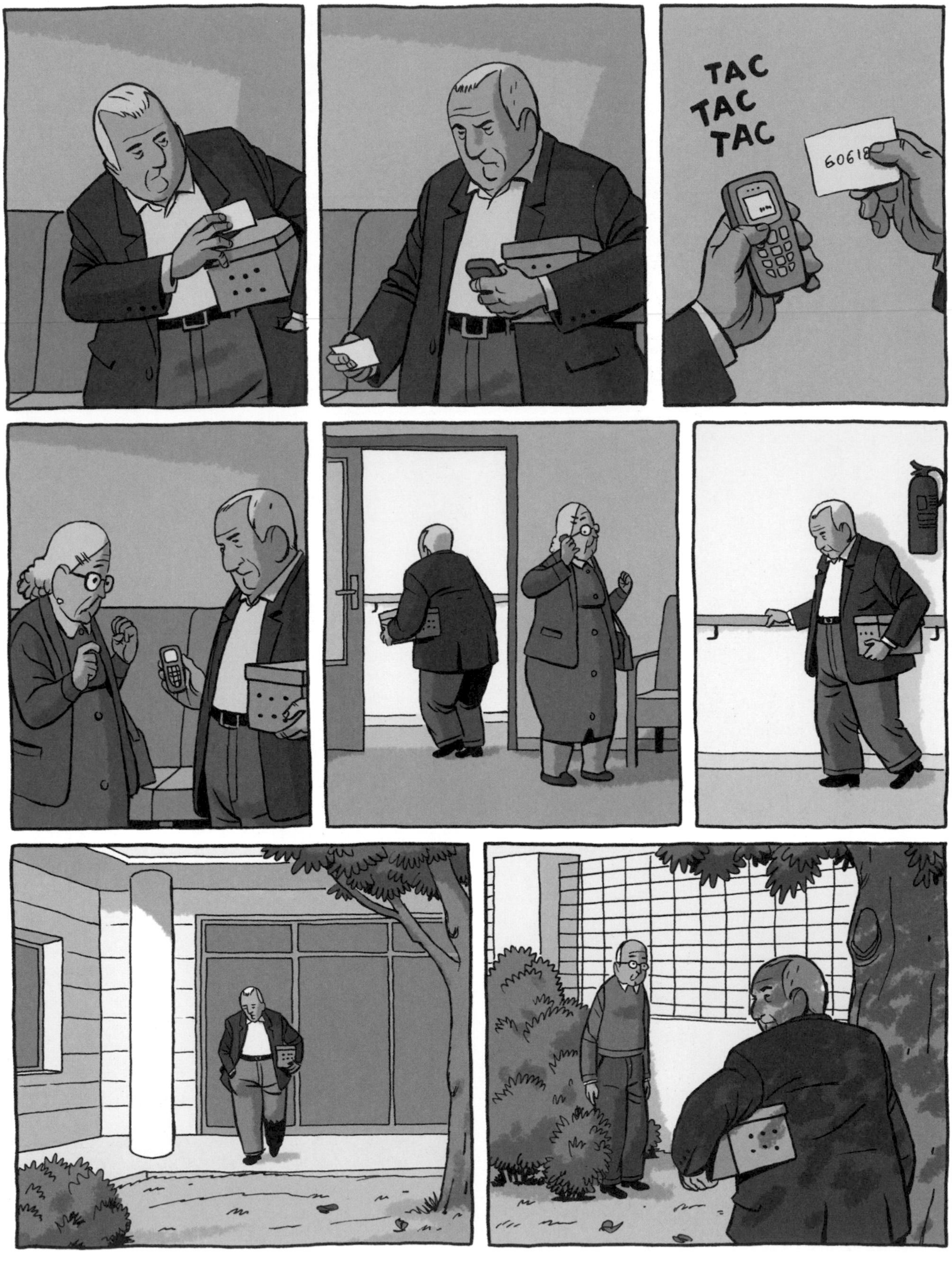
TAC
TAC
TAC
60618

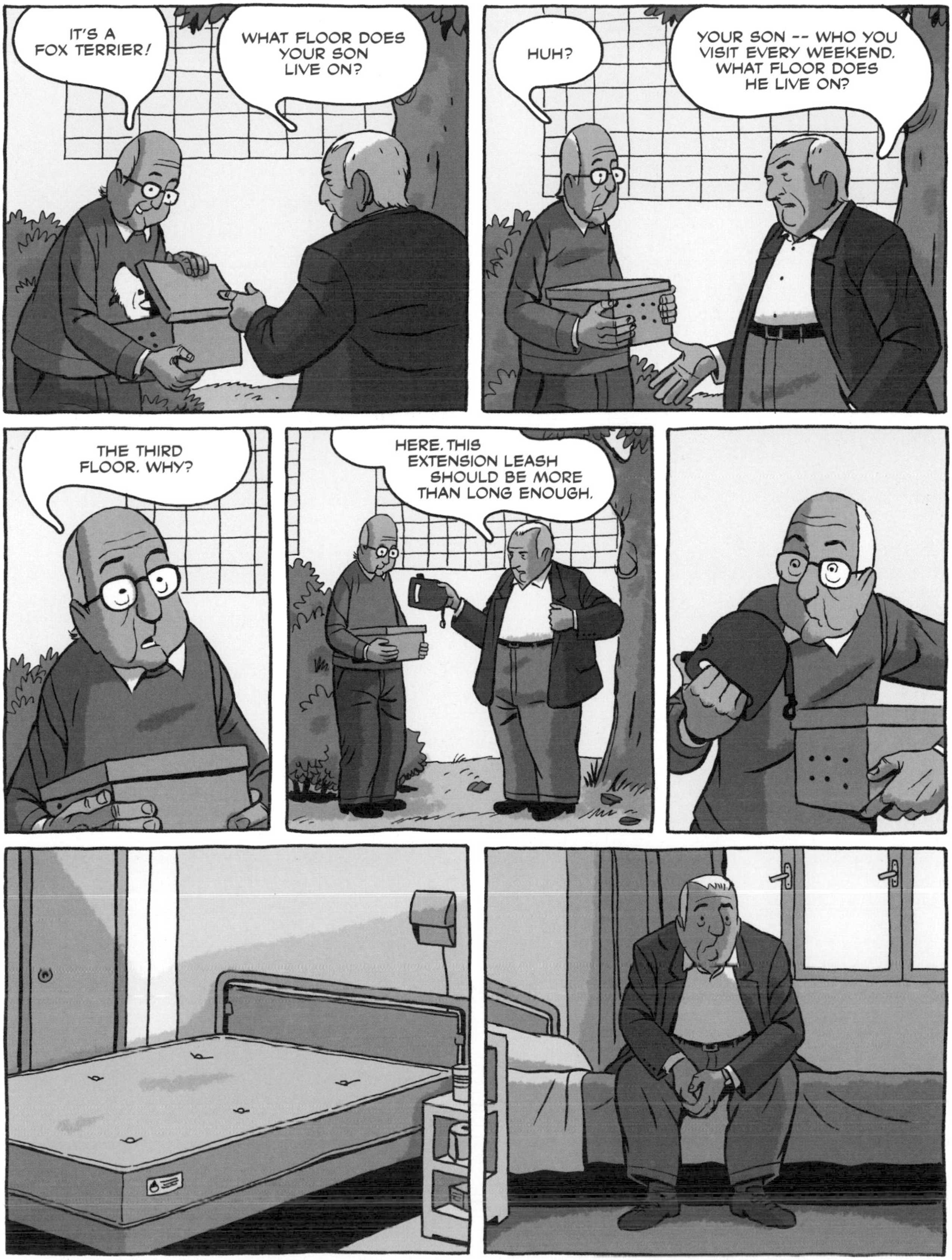
IT'S A FOX TERRIER!
WHAT FLOOR DOES YOUR SON LIVE ON?
HUH?
YOUR SON -- WHO YOU VISIT EVERY WEEKEND. WHAT FLOOR DOES HE LIVE ON?
THE THIRD FLOOR. WHY?
HERE. THIS EXTENSION LEASH SHOULD BE MORE THAN LONG ENOUGH.

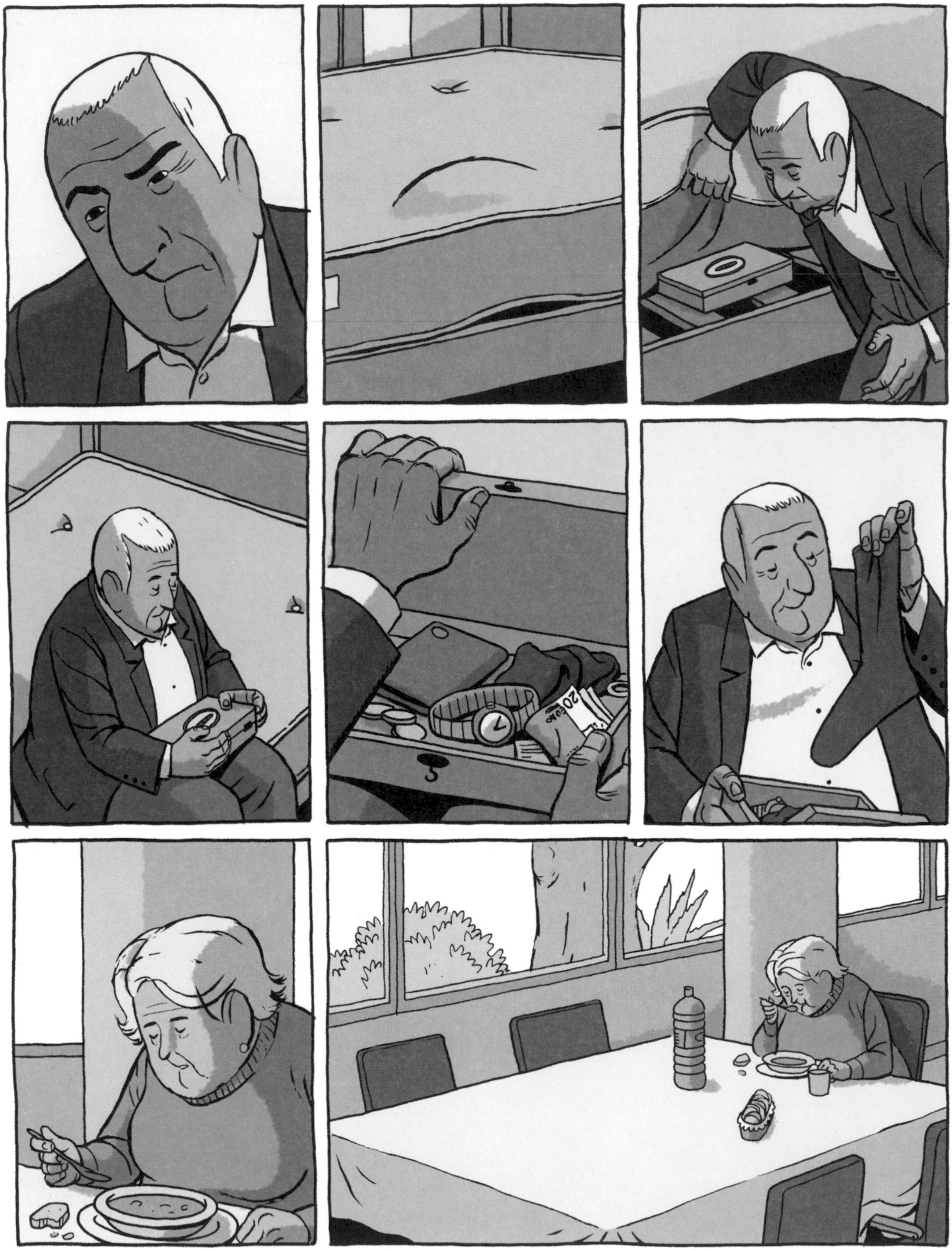

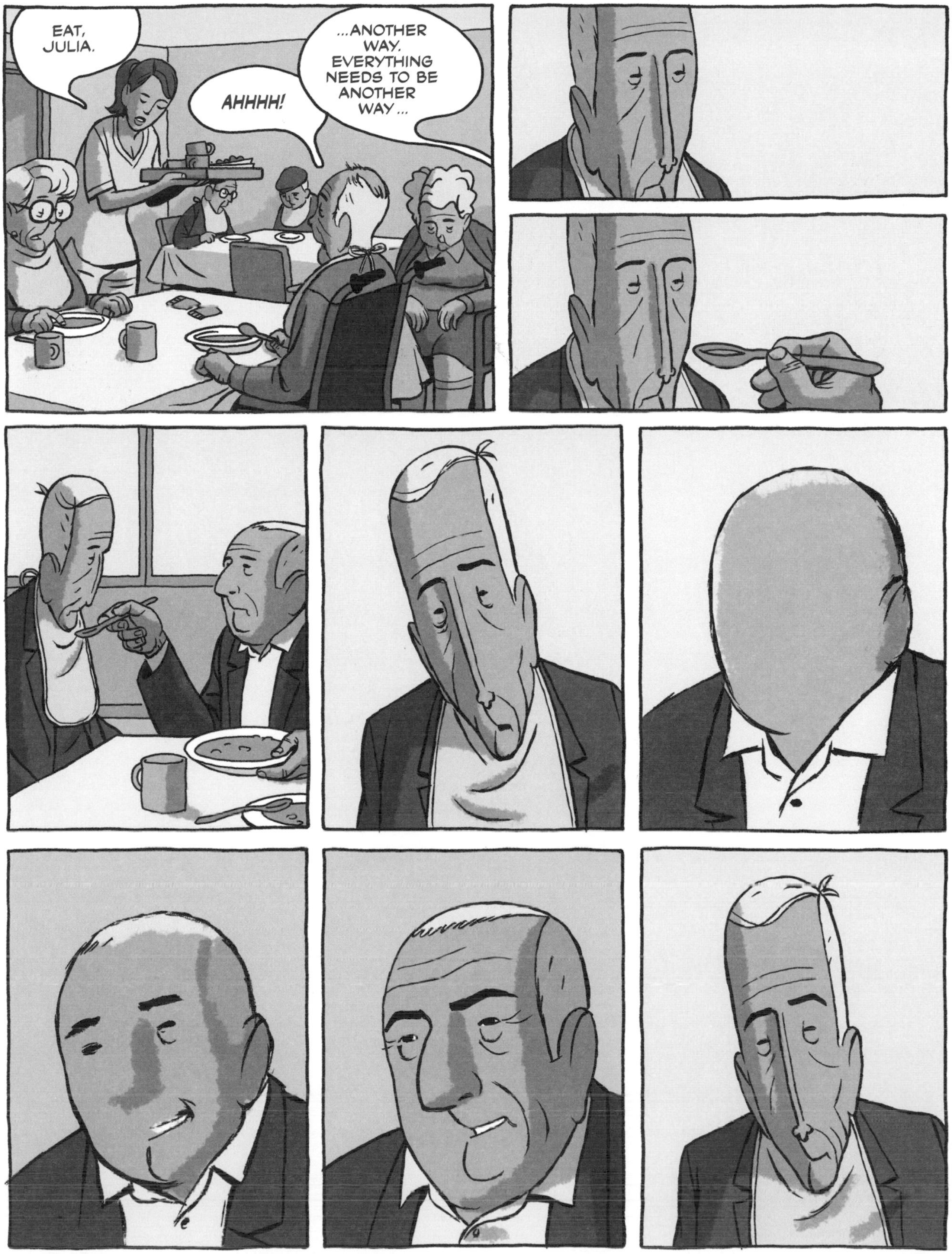
EAT, JULIA.
AHHHH!
...ANOTHER WAY. EVERYTHING NEEDS TO BE ANOTHER WAY...